IN THE NAME OF ALLAH,
THE ALL-BENEFICENT, THE ALL-MERCIFUL

THE SECRET OF PRAYER

(*Sirr us-Salat*)

Imam Khomeini (*s*)

**The Institute for Compilation and Publication of Imam
Khomeini's Works
(International Affairs Department)**

Tables of Contents

Transliteration Symbols

Symbol	Transliteration	Symbol	Transliteration
ء	'	أ	a
ب	b	ت	t
ث	th	ج	j
ح	ḥ	خ	kh
د	d	ذ	dh
ر	r	ز	z
س	s	ش	sh
ص	ṣ	ض	ḍ
ط	ṭ	ظ	ẓ
ع		غ	gh
ف	f	ق	q
ك	k	ل	l
م	m	ن	n
هـ	h	و	w
ي	y	ة	ah
Long Vowels		**Short Vowels**	
آ	a	َ	a
او	u	ُ	u
اى	i	ِ	i
Persian Letters			
Symbol	**Transliteration**	**Symbol**	**Transliteration**
پ	p	چ	ch
ژ	zh	گ	g

Publisher's Note

O

In the Name of Allah, the All-beneficent, the All-merciful

The holy book *"Sirr us-Salat"* is a work of the perfect mystic, the spiritual cod's which was written by Imam Khomeini (*a*) in the year 1358 (lunar year) [19 Khordad 1318 (solar year)].

The book *"Sirr us-Salat"* has been reprinted a few times so far, but as publishers, due to the inaccessibility to the manual main copy, were not able to publish an accepted copy, The Institute for Complication and Publication of Imam Khomeini's (*a*) Works—International affairs department—has published a respectful accepted and perfect copy enjoying, the information lists of different names, locations and necessary items, added with footnotes. The book begins with a letter addressed to Haj Sayyid Ahmad Khomeini, offering the book to him.

More, important, the book has been decorated by the Imam's manual, The Original text. ✍

The Institute for Complication
and Publication of Imam Khomeini's Works

Author's Preface

O

In the Name of Allah, the All-beneficent, the All-merciful
Praise be to God and greetings be peace upon the Messenger of God, may God's
blessing be upon him and his Household (*a*)

This is the testament of an old father who has spent his life idly in ignorance and is now proceeding to the eternal abode with nothing good to his credit but a black list of wrongdoings with hope of pardon by Allah, to a son who is young, involved in world issues and free to choose the divine straight path (may God guide him through His infinite mercy).

My son! The book I am offering to you is a bit of the prayers of the Gnostics and the moral conduct of the peripatetic wayfarers, although my pen is unable to define this itinerary. I confess that all I have written amounts to a few mere words and phrases, and yet I have not been able to catch a spark of this short account myself.

My son! All that lies in this ascension is the utmost ideal of the Gnostics and it is beyond our grasp—"Phoenix is prey to none, gather up to prey the hawk." But we must not be despair of

God's mercy for He is the helper of the weak and support of the indigent. My dear, in the peripatetic journey the word is from creature to Creator, from plurality to unity, and from the earth to beyond the celestial kingdom to the point of absolute annihilation that comes about in the first prostration and annihilation from annihilation which occurs after alertness, in the second prostration. And all this is the Arch of Existence from God and unto God. And, in this state there is no prostrate and no worshipped one— "He is the first and the last, the visible and the unseen."

My son! All that I recommend to you in the first degree is that do not deny the stations of those of Gnostic knowledge for such is the way of the ignorant. And avoid association with those who deny the stations of the pious for they are robbers in the path of God. Leave selfishness and egotism for these are Satan's heritage that, because of his conceit, declined God's declined God's command to bow to His Caliph and chosen one. Know that all of man's miseries emanate from this satanic heritage that is the essential base of the principles of sedition. Perhaps the verse, "Fight them on until there is no more tumult or oppression and Allah's religion reigns supreme," refers in some stages to the grand crusade and fighting the roots of evils, i.e. Satan and its hordes that have spread in men's hearts. From within and without, everyone must himself fight for the eradication of evil and it is this crusade which, if it triumphs all things and people will be set right and corrected.

My son! Try to attain this victory or some of its degrees. Try hard and reduce carnal passions for they are endless. Ask Almighty God for help for without His aid none can get anywhere. The prayer, this ascension of the Gnostics and journey of the lovers, is the way to reach this destination and if you and I succeed to realize one *rakat* of it and see the lights concealed in it and its mysterious secrets, we shall have scented some aspect of the destiny and purpose of God's pious servants and have witnessed a vista of the ascension prayers of the favor and oblige is by His blessing. The road is long and winding, and requires much provision and the provisions of me, and the like of me, are scarce or nil unless the mercy of the Friend, the Glorified one, come to our aid.

My dear! Make good use of the youthful time available to you for all will be lost in old age, even attention to Resurrection and God. One of the tricks of Satan is that he promises the opportunity for self reform and purge in old age so that youthful years may be wasted by negligence and he promises the aged to have long life so that by his false promises men may ignore God until death and at this point he takes away men's faith, if he has not already done so. Therefore, arise to endeavor while you are young and enjoy your strengthen and run away from anything not of God and strengthen your link with Him if you already have one and if, God forbid, you have no link with Him acquire one and strengthen it because no being except Him, the Glorified, is worth having a link with. And the links with His saints, if not meant for Him, are satanic ties and tricks to block the path of Truth from every angle. Do not ever view your conduct with satisfaction. This is how pure devotees were who regarded themselves as nothing and sometimes counted their good points as bad.

My son! The higher the Gnostic station, the higher is the feeling of advancement toward God, after each praising is to be said. As just before entry into the prayers there is *takbir* in glorification of God and *takbir* comes again upon exit from prayers, denoting that God is above and beyond and preeminent to any commendation of attributes and deeds. Truly, who is there to praise the Lord, and what expression is there to praise and who is it to be glorified and by what tongue? For all the worlds from the highest stations in the firmament to the lowest ebb in hell and all in between are nil. Whatever is, is Him, nothing but him has being and what can a non-existent say about the absolute Being? None of the saints would probably mention His name if it were not for His own command and none can disobey Him. For every mention is His mention and as we read, "Your Lord has enjoined you to worship none for help," which is perhaps from God's tongue addressed to all beings and "There is nothing but it praises Him with a eulogy of Him, but you cannot understand their praises." This, too, is in the language of plurality, otherwise He is the Praise and He is the Praised and He is the Praiser. "Indeed, you Lord is performing the prayer" and "God is the light of the heavens and the earth."

My son! Why we who are incapable of thanking Him and His blessings neglect serving His servants? Service to them is service to the Truth or God as all are from Him. In serving the people never consider yourself a creditor, for we are justly indebted to them as they are means by which we serve God. Do not seek name or fame us deep in its pharynx. In serving God's servants choose what is most beneficial to them, not that which best suits yourself or your friends as that is an indication of truthfulness to God.

My dear son! God is ever present and the entire world is His site of presence and the slate of our ego is our record card. Try to choose an occupation that brings you to Him most closely as that is His pleasure. Do not say to me in your heart, "If this is true why are not you like that yourself?" I know I am not endowed with any quality of those of pure heart and I fear this broken pen is at the service of Satan and the polluted ego, and tomorrow I will be accountable for it. But the points raised are factual even by the pen of one like me who am not away from devilish qualities. I take refuge in Almighty God at these last breaths and I hope to receive the intercession of His pious saints.

O God! Hold yourself this decrepit old man and the young Ahmad Threshold by your limitless mercy.

And peace be upon those who follow guidance. ✍

Ruhullah al-Musawi al-Khomeini
Rabi al-Awwal 15, 1407 AH

O

Oh God, lead us to the right humanity way and withhold us from negligence, egoism and perdition and lead us to the circle of the people of Gnostic and knowledge. Remove the veil of egoism I-ness, darkness away from our insight vision as to be united to the real ascension of the people of the prayer and to the four sides of the earth and the heaven we call *takbir*, and we will be shown the mystery secrets as to achieve the sweetness of invoking of the great leader, and lead our hearts' attention merely towards Thyself only, close our eyes to the otherness satanic features and make it focus just upon Thyself. And then, I, the wonderer of the wonder world and negligence and united to the I-ness and egoism, busy with boasting and selfishness unaware of the spiritual stages of the world of existence, I paid sincerity as to write some of the spiritual manners of the holy stages in this spiritual conduct and religious mystic ascension. And myself though have been contented with all the verbal expression and did not gain any high stages, but relating to the following words:

"I like the competent but I am not one of them, Hoping God would allow me prudent, with the name of the Beloved I decorate these pages perhaps this notice, lack of form and meaning is considered as my supplication, makes of the holy men's (*a*) attention towards me who is tangled with desires, and it would be compensated for the rest of my life. It consists of one preface, two texts and one index.

Introduction

And it includes a few chapters

Chapter One:

Know as there are some stages and ranks for human, on some basis, it is known as having two stages: one is the worldly stage and vision and another Hereafter stage and unseen, the former is under the shadow of *rahman* [beneficent] and the latter under the shadow of *rahim* [compassion]. And due to this basis under the shadow and the subordinate the entire names thereabout and Allah is circled by these two names, namely *rahman* and *rahim* [Beneficent and compassion]. As it has been collected in the holy verse:

In the name of God the compassionate the merciful and the gnostics say" "The being has been appeared through the God's names, compassionate and merciful." And these two stages in perfect man from the appearing of the absolute "Will", from the unseen places, up to the withholding material or withholding the seventh heaven which is the human veil, through the great Gnostics—and this is one of the curves of the being—and from the withholding of the emanation up to the ultimate unseen will and the announced being—and this is the second curve—thus the perfect man according to these two calculations, namely the stage vision and appearing to mercifulness and the stage of the unseen stage and appearing to the compassion stage is the whole circle of the existence "Then he drew nigh and came down till he was (distant) two bows' length or even nearer."[1]

And this is one of the realities of the "Holy Night" and it is its secret, because the true sun is within the determination veil. And another is the reality of the Resurrection Day, because it is the time of appearing and it's rising, coming out of the veil, and this is the Divine Day and night.

And upon some basis it possesses three stages" one the worldly stage, the second isthmus, and the third one hereafter and the wisdom stage, and in the perfect man these three stage are: the stage of limited manifestation, the stage of the absolute will-that isthmus and upon on some basis it has the truth of the truths' stage and another is this Oneness of the while names, and in the holy verse "*bismillah*" referred to these three stages" Allah, which is the collective oneness stage, and the name which is the big isthmus, and beneficial and compassioned determinations Will"

And upon some basis it has four stages, realm, heaven, omnipotence, divinity. And upon some basis it has five stages: Absolute testimony, absolute, martyr, absent plus, the stage of the perfect universe according to the quintuple stages usual in the words of Gnostics.

And on some detailed basis it has hundred or thousand stages that description of which is out of the scope of these pages.

Similarly for praying which among the divine ritual is original and commonality, these stages are quite the same and exactly

---

[1] *Surah an-Najm*: 8.

alike because the whale's man spiritual stages based on his spiritual journey from the utmost point of the realm of dissension of worldly realm, which is the desire's injustice abode up to the ultimate real spiritual ascension which is the union to God's annihilation.

And the *buraq* (A fast horse on whom the prophet (*a*) mounted) of the course and the *rafraf* (The name of one of the Messenger's heavenly mounts) of the ascension of the people of the knowledge and the people of the prayer performers and anyone who is in the circle of the divine conduct has got especial prayer unique for oneself and he gains especial pleasure thereof according to one's stage. It goes the same to the ritual of *Hajj* and fasting, though they are behind the range of these prayers.

There are ways lead to God as the number as the breaths of the creatures"[1]

Those who have not achieved such stage there is no such pleasure for them rather the owner of each stage if does not dismount the mount of fury and I-ness, if he denies the other stages, except the stage of his own, and disregards and considers the other stages in vain and redundancy. And this is one the greatest insulations of the spiritual wayfaring and the highest obstacles preventing the promotion of the manner and the spiritual stages that the commanding soul, due to its selfishness and the worldly materials, have been kept within the dark veil and to which the satanic temptation has helped to more go as far as he compares it to holy men's prayers with this own prayer. Or if he gives any advantages he considers the genuflection and some other ritual disciplines as a remarkable point, and if he goes a little further he considers their state of their hearts in the time of the prayer and their understanding of the meaning and

---

[1] *Ilm al-Yaqin*, vol. 1, p. 14.

other subtle points, without knowing the state of the heart's presence and other qualities and their secrets or at least he tries to create the heart up to the measure as he has made up for himself, removing the obstacles and acquires to needed necessary factors.

Though the prayer of the holy men can not be imagined by our impression their prayer, first of all which is the ordinary stage, is the free men's worship and they enjoy special stages and ranks in this spiritual wayfaring about which we'll talk later.

Shortly, there are ranks and stages for the prayer the stage of which differs from the other stages, as the rank of which quite differs from the rank of the other, thus as far as man is in the from of man and is formal man, his prayer is formal, the use of such prayer is only health and physical ritual discipline provided he performs the whole conditions, and the ritual disciplines completely (his prayer) cannot be accepted by the God's court. If he from the apparent stage finds it into the inner stage and comprehends the connotation of which internally and as far as such trend goes on, up to that stage his prayer takes the real form, Rather according to whatever has been said that the prayer is the mount of conduct to the God's way, the matter changes differently, thus, as far as the man's prayer is within the form of mere prayer's frame, has not gone into the inner case and the secret of which has been realized, man is still man and has not been reached the reality thereabout, thus the criterion and the measurement in complement of humanity and reality is the ascension to the real ascending and ascension to the ultimate point of the completion and achieving the union of God's gate through the prayer's stages. Thus it is necessary for the spiritual wayfarer prepares himself for such spiritual and the religious ascension takes with whatever seems necessary and removes all obstacles and insulation coupled with God's soldiers sets out for this journey, while being friend with the God's soldiers and keeps away from Satan and his soldiers who are the robbers of the union. Then he will be saved and keeps on going. And we, from now on, talk about all these soldiers and the other items thereabout.

And our aim and result from this chapter has been summed up in this frame that the prayer, rather the whole worships, enjoys some inner reality apart from this formal apparent case, this it will be realized, and there are many traditions thereabout the description of all of them is out of escape of such limited pages. For example the famous tradition "prayer is the ascension of the pious, that the study of which will clear many meanings for the learned knowledgeable ones from which we have been deprived, and the whole said before has been derived from this tradition.

Imam Sadiq (*a*) said: "There are three types of praying: Some people worship God because they have fear, this is a slave type, some people worship for getting something is return these are the wage-receivers, and some worship God for love, these are liberated ones, and this is the best worshipping.[1]

In *Wasail*, Shaykh Sadiq quoted from Imam Sadiq (*a*): "People perform the God's worshipping in three forms: Some people for gaining blessing, these are the greedy ones and their deed is avarice, and another group are frightened by fire, this is fear and not worship, and I worship God for his love this is the worship of the generous ones and this is immune and he said.

"Whoso bringeth a good deed will have better than its worth, and such are safe in the fire. Are ye reward aught save what ye did?[2]

In *Nahj al-Balaghah* there is the same similar tradition:

---

[1] *Wasail ash-Shariah*, vol. 1, p. 45.
[2] *Surah an-Naml*: 89.

"Worship God as though you see Him, then if you don't see him he sees you" and whomever God like is of the rescuer ones."[1]

And this refers to two stages of presence before the Beloved—as it will come later—and quoted of that majesty "Verily two of my followers stand for performing prayer, they bow the same and genuflected the same while there is a big gap from earth to sky between their prayers.

It has been quoted of Ali (*a*) "Happy is the one who praises for the God's sake sincerely, and what his heart's eyes sees and to what he hears neither regret not sad and also whatever he gets not should not be sorrowful. We talk about it later.

Then by studying this holy tradition and searching in the deeds of the holy Imams (*a*) we find them trembling, pale worried, and fearful while preparing for the prayer, before prayer, even some of them fainted, forgot themselves and thought entirely of God, then it should be quite evident that the reality and the importance of this prayer, this divine worship is a remedy for being free from the small cage of the nature predicaments and hardships. As the prayer is not just some formality deeds and observing some repeating actions. We end this debate by this holy tradition for whom: "Lo! There in verily is a reminder for him who has a heart, or giveth ear with full intelligence.[2]

From the book *Falah as-Sail* written by Ibn-e Tawus (*a*) has been quoted that it has been said: "Tradition *Rizam*, the freed slave Khalid Ibn Abdullah who was at the present of Abu Jafar Mansur Dawaniqi asked Imam Jafar (*a*) about the prayer and its description. He replied: "Prayer possesses four thousand disciplines that you are notable to perform even one of them. *Rizam* said: "Tell me and performing and observing the religious

---

[1] *Khisal*, p. 188.
[2] *Surah Qaf*: 37.

duty and all. In this case and by expressing this holy tradition to the men of cognition and compare it with the prayer's principal, it would take time and we refer to some of its fractions later on, maybe! And if four thousand structures which Imam Sadiq (*a*) had uttered, about the formal cases and ceremonies, you would not have been able to perform even one single of the whole yes, breaking tendencies of others, except God, and approaching God almighty, leaving others and joining God's followers and sacrificing oneself for God is not possible except for the men of knowledge, the real men of spiritual wayfarers and the intimate ones.

"*Fatuba lahum thumma tuba lahum wa hanyian li arbab-e naimi naimuhum.*"

A real suitable, accepted prayer which prevents the man from all vices—the tradition is not finished and continues.[1]

Chapter Two:

It is quite clear for the learned ones that the man, the spiritual wayfarer's prayer is different, his rituals is different from the perfect man who has reached the ultimate goal and touches the spiritual stage—the stage that the spiritual wayfarer, is on its way. The *salik*, spiritual wayfarer's prayer, as far as travelers, namely while traveling, his prayer is for union, and after achieving the union stage his prayer is for the vision of the Beloved and the Beloved's charm, without changing his main rituals and deeds. As the researchers and Gnostics believe the reasonable realm comparing to the world, though the high point has no any relation to the low, point their impression about this world a simple word and ordinary common term is that under the

---

[1] *Falah as-Sail*, p. 23.

affection and being inspired by the divine worship and the manifestations of names. Attribute and essence. In short, the observed ones by vision of the Beloved beauty gain the invisible manifestation, which finds expression in their hearts enthusiastically according to the sort of praying they perform. And though they have no any intention upon none of qualities independently, their ritual disciplines are unchanged formally, without increasing or decreasing, and follows the religious rule accurately, as the Holy Prophet (s) due to the vision of the greatness of light while was praying in ascending night, and the realization of manifestation essence and the absent essence he prostrated and fainted that we will refer to it later.

And like this spiritual attraction and annihilation totally is the same as the lovers and his loving behaviors which is out of control because none of the actions of him is quite unintentional.

There is no before hand rule and written regulation for loving affairs because love by itself is fire, it burns, it shines and radiates out of the lover's heart and expands overall vastly and deeply, this is incentive enough for loving affairs, this is the best means for the lover, from the jar seeps out through whatever contained within the jar.

So, it is a must for the spiritual wayfarer to act very seriously to rid his knowledge and rites of the intrusion of Satan and the commanding soul and to go deep into his doing, quests and desire.

And also being absorbed in the stage Divinity and being in love with the feature of Him, the Beloved's inner manifestation and the Beloved benevolent qualities which manifests in his visible world and it finds its own expression in his martyr state, this is the whole frame work and outline of the prayer. If there would be anything else except the case which occurs to the messenger (a), the real observed and the real united, that case is the satanic case and the wayfarer is standing firm in his own egoism and I-ness. He has to try to rescue himself and leaves the miserable course.

Thus, some sort of praying which has been related to some of the theologies called "silent prayer" and a very especial manner *alif* of Allah is pronounced, then *la* with a long hesitation and then *ha* and it goes further to five which makes the figure five altogether supposing it would have been correct, the fool was the one who invented such foolish rule.

Shortly, it is worth nothing and it has nothing to with the prophet (*a*), as an in vain meaningless mixture, to which should not be paid any attention at all. And our Gnostics the perfect Shaykh the honorable Shah-Abadi (*a*) said: "All prayers are confined in this frame namely conveying the God's praising into the nature and the inner side of man. And in this course while there is pleasure for the heart, for the mind similarly there is some pleasure, as well, for the body which is these rituals.

Thus fasting is the God's praising and the manifestation of his praising, confessing his divinity, and similarly the prayer which enjoys the stage of oneness is the praising of the sacred essence through all names and attributes.

Thus from the above discussion it is understood that the prayer is the ascension and as wayfarer's means and after having reached this journey which is quite in vain and meaningless because it is against the wayfarer's conduct and against the people of the heart. Such thought has been produced by the ill-mind of some personalities who were not aware of the knowledge of the divine affairs, we protect to God almighty.

Chapter Three:
[In the expressing the secret of prayer concisely]

As it is obvious prayer, due to its heavenly feature, consists of supplication intonation recital though according to its real form and formal form enjoys united case and conformity, and as nearer to the perfection points, more united it becomes, as up to the ultimate degree of perfection in which there is the union of the great Resurrection. And after this, we will refer to this point, God willing. And the formal worldly union follows the union of the formal absent one, as it is fixed in its own place. And the perfect of the formal worldly union is in the annihilation within the inner of the heaven, it is explained as the great Resurrection. And there are mystery secrets for each one of the ritual, as there is in the holy tradition:

Shaykh Hurr al-Amili (*a*) in the "*al-Wasail*" on behalf of the book *Uyun Akhbar ar-Rida* and quoted the Imam Rida (*a*) saying that he said: "As a matter of fact the real prayer consists of two parts, and for some, only one part there is and for the other, two parts (*rakat*) have been added and to some parts nothing has been added. The main reason is that principally prayer is only one part, because the main prayer is a single figure one, but as the God almighty know the servants are not able to perform even that one single part—which is the least—and won't approach it, he organized and added one more part to it as to the second part would be a complementary part for the first part.[1]

Chapter Four:

---

[1] *Uyun Akhbar ar-Rida*, vol. 2, p. 107, part 34, tradition 1.

[On expressing the presence of the heart and its stages]

Though it was more about that here it should have been explained the expressions of the heart condition to the learned and the scholars and to the knowledgeable ones and to the jurisprudent and to the theologian through Quran but as I found it of no use in this matter and it was a very long discussion, I have put it aside and focused upon the presence of the heart and its stages.

It is not hidden to the knowledgeable insightful learned scholars aware of the secret of the data of his infallible (*a*) that the real sense of worshipping and its perfect details depend on the presence of the heart without which no worship will be accepted by the divine court and such worship has no value at all.

We will refer to some traditions in the next chapters. And because the perfection, the defection, the illumination and the gloominess of each creature finds its expression in its recent perfection and his recent conditions and the man's perfection, defection and his cruelly are evaluated through the perfection and defection of essence of humanity which is the divine breath and his single spirit similarly the absolute worship especially prayer, which is one the principals of the heaven having been created and purified by God that its perfection, defection, illumination and the darkness of which depend on and the unseen spirit and divine breath that has been inspired through the essence of humanity.

The more sincerity and the purification of heart-which are the two principals of the prayer—the exalted spirit therein will be cleaner and more perfect. And the perfection of the holy men's deeds and infallibles' deeds were not merely for bestowing some pieces of bread and their helps, rather their deeds were inspired by the inner causes and the illumination of their actions, as there is in holy verse which says: We only seek the God's satisfaction and nothing else."

Rather a single stroke of Ali (*a*) is superior to the whole worships performed by all men and the pixies. This value is not because of the worldly deeds, rather it was due to the nature of the deed no matter whoever would has done it, would have had the some value as well, though it was so important because of the outcome of the action after which the enemies escaped, otherwise the army of the Islam would have had a bitter aftermath and defeated but the sincerity of the action and the presence of the heart in this divine task had the major role. And it is known that when Ali (*a*) got angry because of the misdeeds of that evil, Ali (*a*) was withheld from his killing through the divine aspect as to not be said: "He killed him for his own sake as Ali (*a*) was angry" The matter of egoism was over in that process.

And though the anger of that great man the guardianship of God is the absolute God's anger, he made his action pure and sincere and annihilated himself to God thoroughly, his deed in fact is beyond the evaluation and should not be compared it with anything else. And we will refer to it God willing in some other occasion. And now we write about the presence of the heart and there are some stages for it which we refer to them briefly.

Thus, the first stage of the presence of the heart related to the worships, is the presence of the heart generally, entering to this stage is possible for everyone. And the point is that man has to make his own heart understand that the worshipping phrase is the second step for praising the Beloved. And from the beginning till the end of it, generally speaking man should make his heart understand that it should be busy praising the Beloved and make his heart ready for this case, though he himself does not know what sort of praising he is reciting, or what names he is calling and so on. He is not aware how he is praising the God almighty and what sort of praising he is performing, whether this praising in essentials or nominal or else. It is the same that a poet reads a sonnet for somebody and makes a child understand that this is praising so called! Though the child is unaware of different between praising and the praised and in generally who is who and which is which that debate. He only knows praising and that is all. The same goes to the school children who would recite the Muhammad's Gnostic by heart—being inspired to them—without knowing the concept of which and know not why they are reading that sort of things. But it is for the first time that their heart touches such words and they are talking with the tongue of the noble men's expression. They taste sweet taste with those dates.

In short, in invoking and intonation or the prayer's rituals and disciplines, the intention of praising and worshipping through the tongue of the origin, namely in some cases the God almighty and in some cases the prophet (*a*), for some people like us whose secret has not been purified and their tendencies are connected to the non-divinity which will be referred to it, God willing.

The second degree, which is lower in rank, is that the wayfarer himself present in His presence and observes the discipline of the presence and company. The Messenger of Allah (*s*) says: "If you can be of those who are in the first degree, then worship Allah accordingly, or else, do not neglect the fact that you are in the presence of the Lord." Naturally, there is a discipline for being in the presence of Allah, which should not be neglected in respect of the state of servitude. In a tradition, Abu Hamzah ath-Thumali narrates: "I saw Ali ibn al-Husayn (*a*) performing his prayer. His cloak slipped off his shoulders, but he did not try to rearrange it until he finished the *salat*. When I asked him about that, he said: "Woe unto you! Do you know at whose service I was?"[1]

The Messenger of Allah (*s*) was quoted to have said: "Two of my followers stand for the prayers, and, although their genuflection and suspiration are the same, the difference between the two prayers is like that which is between the earth and the sky."

He also said: "Is the person who turns his face in the prayer not afraid that it may turn into the face of an ass?"[2]

He further said: "Whoever performs a two-*rakat* prayer without paying attention to any worldly matter, Allah, the Exalted, will forgive him his sins.

In another *hadith* he said: "A prayer half of it may be accepted, or one-third, or a quarter, or one-fifth, or even one-tenth. Another prayer may be folded, like an old dress, and be thrown back at the face of its owner."

"No part of the prayer is yours except that part which you perform with an attentive heart."[3]

Imam al-Baqir (*a*) has quoted the Messenger of Allah (*s*) as saying: "When a believing servant stands for the prayer Allah, the Exalted, looks at him (or he said: He turns to him) until he finishes, and mercy shadows over his head, the angels surround him from all sides up to the horizon of the heaven, and Allah assigns an angel to stand at his head, saying: "O *musalli*, if you

---

[1] *Wasail ash-Shiah*, vol. 4, "*Book of as-Salat*," see on "The acts of *as-Salat*," ch. 3, *hadith* 6, p. 688.

[2] *Bihar al-Anwar*, vol. 81, "*Book of as-Salat*," ch. 16, *hadith* 41, p. 249.

[3] *Mustadrak al-Wasail*, "*Book of as-Salat*," sec. on "*The acts of the Salat*," ch. 2, *hadith* 20.

know who is looking at you, and to whom you are supplicating, you will look to nowhere, nor will you leave your position."[1]

Imam as-Sadiq (*a*) is quoted to have said: "Eagerness and fear will not get together in a heart unless Paradise is his. So when you perform your prayer, turn with your heart to Allah, the Glorified, the Almighty, because there would be no believing servant who would turn with his heart to Allah, the Exalted, during the prayer and invocation unless Allah would turn to him the hearts of the believers, and with their love He would back him and lead him to paradise."[2]

It is narrated that Imams al-Baqir and as-Sadiq (*a*) said: "Nothing of your prayer is yours except that which you did with an attentive heart. So, if one performed it completely mistaken, or neglected its disciplines, it would be folded and thrown back at its owner's face.[3]

Imam Baqir al-Ulum (the cleaver of knowledge) (*a*) is quoted to have said: "of a servant's ascends half, one-third, one-fourth or one-fifth to his account. That is, of his prayer will not ascend except that part which is performed with an attentive heart. We have been commanded to perform the *nafilah* so as to make up for the shortcomings of the obligatory prayer.[4]

Imam as-Sadiq (*a*) is quoted to have said: "When you wear the ihram for the prayer (i.e., when you prepared for the prayer), pay attention to it, because when you pay attention to it, Allah will pay attention to you. If you do not care for it, Allah will not care

---

[1] *Mustadrak al-Wasail*, "*Book of as-Salat*," sec. on "*The acts of the Salat*," ch. 2, *hadith* 22.
[2] *Wasail ash-shiah*, vol. 4, "*Book of as-Salat*", sec. on "The acts of the *Salat*," ch. 3, *hadith* 3, p. 678.
[3] *Ibid*, *hadith* 1.
[4] *Mustadrak al-Wasail*, "*Book of as-Salat*," sec. on "The acts of the *Salat*," ch. 3, *hadith* 7.

for you. So, sometimes, does not ascend of the prayer except one-third, one-fourth or one-sixth, according to the amount of attention the *musalli* pays to it. Allah grants nothing to the negligent.

The Messenger of Allah (s) is quoted to have said to Abu Dharr: "Two moderate parts of prayer with contemplation are better than worshipping a whole night with a negligent heart. The traditions on this are many, but those which have been related are enough for those whose hearts are awake and attentive.

One may have the notion that without purifying the outside of his kingdom he can reach the state of the truth of humanity, or he can purify his inner heart, as this will be a Satanic vanity and of Satan big tricks. This is because the heart's impurity and darkness will be increased by disobediences, which mark the triumph of nature over spirituality. Unless the wayfarer conquers the kingdom of the outside, he will remain deprived of inner conquests, which are the big objective, and no way will be opened for him to happiness. Thus, one of the big obstacles of this wayfarer is the impurities of the acts of sincere repentance.

After nominal manifestation, some example of essential manifestation which is the ultimate stage of the presence of the Beloved in heart will occur. And it too enjoys some ranks and as we are a veiled from some of the stages of the presence of heart, therefore we cut it short, we talk had better talk about the primary presence of the heart perhaps we'll get a better result thereabout.

Chapter Five:
[About the presence of heart's stage]

Having been known the presence of heart's stages, it is better and much important is than man should try hard to cure his soul and if he is unable and is out of acquiring of the whole stages at least acquires some of the stages or a few of them, beneath the high stages.

It should be known that the source of the heart's presence is within the frame of action and the cause and attention of the soul to it, is that the heart considers that action an important case and put it into consideration and really take it serious. Telling an example makes the matter more understandable:

If you are invited to a court meeting a king, as he is an important personality to you, your heart considers him important you pay full attention on everything precisely, you have a real presence of heart but on the contrary if you are invited by an ordinary people you won't enjoy such presence of heart like the time you had at the court of the king. This makes clear why our heart is lack of real presence while worshipping and praising have been done normally.

If we take serious our praising with God as serious as we talk to an ordinary person and take the former case so serious case the same as the latter, we won't be involved in such negligence and forgetting. And it is so obvious that such laxity and shirking derives from the faith weakness to the God Almighty and the prophet (*a*) and the tradition of the infallible, rather this indulgence is derived from the Lordship and the divinity sacred stage, but the master who has invited us to praise though the tongue of holy men (*a*) and the messengers (*a*) rather through his own sacred Quran and has opened the way of intercourse despite all of these, we don't observe principles with God as we observe toward an ordinary weak person, rather when we start praying, which is the main gate of the presence of divinity and his court, we get scattered mind and all the evil thoughts suddenly launch an attach into our mind and we think about many other things but God, as though the prayer is the key of the shop or the abacus or the pages of the book. It is nothing but the faith weakness, the weakness of believing, and if man would understand the aftermath of such shirking and the defect of this indulgent and makes his heart understand, of course he finds a remedy and tries to behave himself.

If one not takes some affairs great and serious, little by little he gives it up, and giving up the religious discipline leads to give up the religion entirely and we explained this in the book *"Sharh-e Arbain."*

If one makes one's heart aware of the importance of this shirking one becomes aware and awakes up from the heavy sleep. Oh dear, think a little about your own state and refer to the tradition quoted of the infallible (*a*), try to make your soul understand that this ritual, and especially the prayer, and more important than that the religious rituals are the source of prosperous in both "worlds", the perfections in this world and salvation in hereafter.

According to the many traditions in different chapters about the vision and reason of the people of recovering and forms for each of the accepted worship, unseen forms which helps human in all cases invisibly and the matter of imagination of the deeds is one of the affairs that should be considered so obviously and both wisdom and narration have the same opinion thereabout. And such unseen form follows the heart's presence and its attention and the worship lack of the heart's attention is invalid and won't be accepted by the Allah's court and we refer to few verses thereabout which is adequate:

Ah, woe unto worshippers, who are heedless of their prayer[1]— Successful, indeed are the believers who are humble in their prayers.[2]

---

[1] *Surah al-Maun*: 4-5.
[2] *Surah al-Muminun*: 1-2.

It should also be noted that all the external and internal powers which Allah, the Exalted, has bestowed upon us from the invisible world are divine deposits free from all impurities and are purged and purified, and even illuminated with the light of the God-given disposition, and excluded from Satan's dark and impure influence. Yet, since they have descended in the dark abode of the world of nature, and the influential hands of the devil of imagination and fancy have reached them, they have deviated from the original purity and primary disposition, and got polluted with diverse Satanic filths and impurities. So, if the wayfarer to Allah could, by adhering to the outside and return the divine trusts as they had been given to him with no treason, he would be forgiven and protected, and, as far as the outside is concerned, he need not worry, and then he would turn to the second kind of impurity, which is more corrupt and more difficult to cure, and thus, it is more important to the people of austerity, because as long as the inner moralities of the soul are corrupt and encircled by spiritual impurities, it will not deserve the state of holiness and "the private place of intimacy" as the origin of the corruption of the exterior kingdom of the soul is its corrupt morals and its vile habits. And, unless the wayfarer changes his vile habits to good ones, he will not be safe from the evil acts. If he is successful in repentance (while still having vile habits), its stability—which is a matter of grave importance—cannot be achieved. So, the outer purification depends on the inner purification, besides the fact that the interior impurities cause deprivation of happiness, and originate the Hell of morals, which, as the people of knowledge say, is word and more intense in burning than the Hell of deeds. This question had frequently been mentioned in the traditions of the infallible (a).

Therefore, it is a must for the wayfarer to Allah to carry out this purgation. After he has cleansed his soul of the corrupting impurities of the morals with the pure water of useful knowledge and lawful, good austerity, he will have to set upon purifying the heart, the capital which, if reformed, all kingdoms will be reformed, and if it is corrupt, all will be corrupt. The impurities of the world of the heart are the origin of all impurities, such as being attached to other than Allah, to oneself and to this world. This is originated by the love of this world, which is at the head of all sins, and by self-love, which is the mother of all diseases. As long as the roots of this love are still deep in the heart of the wayfarer, he will see no marks of the love of Allah in it, and he will find no way to his destination and objective. So, as long as there are remnants of this love in the heart, his journey will not be to Allah, but to the self, to the world, and to Satan. So, being purged of the love of self and of the world is the first stage of purifying the journey would not be to Allah, and it would be a sort of carelessness to refer to wayfarer and in this instance.

After this stage there are other stages, after which there will appear a model of Attar's Seven Cities of love, the recite of which, as a wayfarer, could see himself at the bend of a lane, while we remain behind walls and thick veils, and think that those "cities" and "kings" are nothing but of the weavings of our presumption. I have nothing to do with Shaykh Attar or Maytham at-Tammar, but I do not deny the original Gnostic stations, and I cordially love their owners, and, by this love, I hope to be relieved. You yourself be whom you may, and bind yourself to whom you like.

But I do not approve of disloyalty by brethren in faith and by spiritual friends to the Gnostic friends, and I will not refrain from offering advice, which is the right of the believers to one another.

At the top of the spiritual impurities, which cannot be purged even with the seven seas, and which caused despair to the great prophets (*a*), is the impurity of "the compound ignorance", which is the origin of the incurable disease of denying the stations of the people of Allah and of knowledge, and is the source of doubting the people of the heart. As long as man is polluted with such impurities, he will not take a step towards knowledge or rather, this impurity so often extinguishes the inborn light of disposition, which is the light for the road of guidance, and puts out the fire of love, which is the heavenly horse for ascending to high stations, causing man to eternally stick to the earth of nature.

Therefore, it is necessary for man, through thinking about the status of the prophets and the perfect holy men, and by contemplating their stations, to wash those impurities away from his heart, and not to be satisfied with the status he is in, because this satisfaction with the knowledge one has, and remaining stagnant, are of the great tricks Satan and the evil-commanding soul. We take refuge in Allah from them. Now, as this thesis is written according to the taste of the common people, I refrain from the three purifications of the holy men. And praise be to Allah.

Shaykh, the perfect Gnostic Shah-Abadi said: "Man while invoking should be like the one who is teaching a child the first childish words and tries to make the child imitate as to be fluent in speaking similarly when a person is invoking he should make his heart imitate. And as far as one talks in the tongue of invoking and teaching his heart imitates the appearance helps the inner and as soon as the word is repeated he becomes happy and this makes his tiredness abolish then first of all, teacher helps the child and then the child himself tries and achieves the goal, it goes similarly to the prayer, of course it be becomes natural and the praising and worshipping becomes ordinary task like some other affairs.

Chapter Six:
[On the affairs which help one acquiring the presence of the heart]

And there some affairs in praying that from now on in its suitable place we refer to it. And now in a general way for the absolute worship we discuss. And that is the human's inner and outer affairs the most important of which is the heart's affairs that must be cut. And the heart's main affairs are the world and the worldly material. If man pays his main attention upon the acquiring the worldly affairs merely and intends to compile the wealth, the heart is driven to that point and it becomes its main attraction land if one thing is left out the other one appears there and keeps the heart busy will itself.

The example of heart is like a bird which is flying from one branch to another branch all the time. As long as there is the worldly desires in our heart the heart's bird belongs to its branches, and if he observes austerity and practices and thinks about the future of his misdeeds and the process life of the infallible and the God's noble, he will cut the tree, then the heart becomes calm and will be able to absorb the completions that one of which is the heart's presence and its stages, the more he tries to reduce the heart's attention toward the worldly material the more success for achieving his goal he gains.

And if one thinks a little about the outcome of the worldly people and the world lovers and the corruption done by them and the defames which have been remained by them making the pages of the history black, all are derived from the longing for the wealth and high position and totally the worldly tenderness, and the decay which is against it, there would be punishment in the hereafter, he will confess by any means and at any cost and through any austerity and ascetics which is possible the abortion from the heart's core and removal of this gloom and darkness which is necessary, and this can be achieved by some measures.

Though giving up fully cannot be fulfilled by no one, but the reduction and the cutting of that branches and leaves is quite possible, rather it is easy.

And of course if one does not take the worldly material as the one's main object he may divide his thought and his heart thus through such manner he may purify the heart for praying. And perhaps he tries for sometimes looking after his heart and withholds himself, he may get the good result and gradually he will be able to uproot the root of such corruption and decay.

And it should be known the heinous world which is uttered by the infallible is in fact the love for the world and the material— namely worldly materials—otherwise the world itself of a vision is one of the manifestation of the God's vision, and the centre for the training the infallible Gnostic, scholars and the theologians, and it is a place for completing the sacred divine affairs for men and the landing field for the hereafter, and it is one of the most important places for the vision of the knowledgeable ones Many a time that somebody is lack of enjoying the spiritual world and because of his love to the worldly affairs he will be one of the worldly one and the forgiver of God and the Resurrection, and the other who possesses kingdom, wealth and power, like Solomon—the son of David but he is not the one of the worldly lovers, and he would be a divine religious devotee. And it is clear that it has nothing to do with the worldly affairs and loving of the world. Many a lovers of the world are empty handed and simultaneously are poor and indigent and those wealthy lack of love of the world who distinguished between this world and the hereafter became prosperous.

Referring to this point it has been mentioned in the traditions quoted to Imam Sajjad (*a*): "There are two kinds of the world, the world which is evil[1] and some world has been condemned due to the worldly lovers or spending time for removing the love thereof.

Shortly whatever withholds the man from achieving union to Allah and gains the perfection is the world loving which deprives man from enjoying the worship and supplication, more than that it makes the heart dark and gloomy. In the holy tradition it is concerned the head of all the sins. And there are so many traditions about it that it won't suitable in such a small scope, we'll refer to it God's willing. And after having reduced the heart's affairs, it must reduce the outer affairs similarly, the religious ritual is mostly for such special occasion, such as: avoid looking round, playing with hands, touching the beard, watching the pictures drown on the carpet and so many other in vain actions even Shaykh Said, Shaykh Martyr Second (*a*) in the book the secret of the prayer says: "For the person who is unable to concentrate pay attention on the slightest article around him or as soon as his eyes happens to catch a glimpse of something he diverts his concentration from the praying he had better close his eyes, or prays in a dark place, or standing in front of a wall as not to see his surroundings, he has to avoid praying on the carpet with different colored painting, or he had better pray in a small place so small that has room only for one person, as he can concentrate on his praying.

For the devotees it is suitable first of all to look after their sincerity of their hearts, more over they should themselves distinguish that praying should be performed either in proving or as a whole apparently according to the tranquility and readiness of the prayer, thank God...

---

[1] *Usul al-Kafi*, p. 4.

The Primary Text on Preparing the Prayer and in a few Chapters

Chapter One:
[Concerning the purifier]

As it was referred before there are stages for the prayer according to the stages and the ranks of the spiritual wayfarers, similarly there are some conditions and disciplines for preparing the prayer that should be observed. In this stage very shortly are bring an example that comparing with some other conditions there would be no need of repeating.

Thus, the purifying of the formal prayer and the form of purifying with water the secret of life and the soil which is the ultimate of manifestation before the knowledgeable people.

And the purifying of the people of the faith is the apparent purification from the sins and lust and fury. And the purification of the people of the inner side is the purifying from the spiritual faith and purifying from the misdeed manners. And the purification of the true people and it is the purification of the satanic temptations and purifying from the thoughts it is the purification of the Satan behaviors the harmful and in vain thoughts and the purification of the people of the heart, it is the purifying from becoming variegated, and the purification of the people of mystery, it is the covering of vision. And the purification of the people of kindness and the absorbed ones to avoid of praying attention to otherness. And the purification of the people of the guardianship, it is the purifying from the vision and expecting the ranks and the stages and the purification of the extremes and grudges the soldiers of Satan are on the opposite side, but as the divine aspects have mastery over the satanic aspects, at the beginning, man's disposition possesses natural divine light, safety and happiness, as is openly stated in the noble traditions and hinted at in the noble divine Book.[1] As long as man is in this world, he can, on his own free will, put himself at the disposal of either of the two. So, if from the beginning of the God given disposition till the end, Satan had no way of intruding, man would be divine, luminous from head to foot with purity and happiness, his heart being the light of Allah, observing nothing but Allah. His inward and outward powers would be luminous and pure, and no one would use them but Allah, and Satan would have no share in them, nor would his soldiers be able to control him.[2]

And the purification of the people of sobriety after self-unconsciousness. And it should be known that for each of the prayer for the spiritual wayfarer there is a needed purifying especial case for that particular prayer without that purification praying is impossible and also praising is invalid as in the holy

---

[1] For example, the noble verse: "So set to the face to the religion, as a man of pure faith-Allah's nature upon which He originated mankind." (*Surah ar-Rum* 30:30). See the *hadith* in *Bihar al-Anwar*, vol. 3, p. 276; vol. 64, p. 130, and in *at-Tawhid*, ch. 53, p. 321.

[2] *The Discipline of the Prayer*, Imam Khomeini (*a*), p. 35.

verse: which one touched save the purified [*Surah al-Waqiah*: 79]

No one touches its apparent except the purified and its inner except the people of the inner purified, and its secrets except the confidant, then no one reaches the prayer of the inner side except those who wash their hands and their faces by the fountain of cordial life and through which touches from the head up to the foot's fingers, being purified ready to go to the friend's abode, and we from now on shortly explain about the infallibles prayer and the learned people God's willing.

And now we write about some points that it is necessary to know for the especial noble ones. And that is the God Almighty who has emphasizes upon the purification of clothes and body and he considers purification part of faith and observes the purified discipline in all affairs such as dealing, relationship, and any other behaviors and also about the clothes which does not belong to man, he emphasized that the purification of which is the needed condition for the praying. Rather referring to the divine book and the traditions quoted of messengers and the infallible will be understood that the purification of the hearts is much more important than that the purification of appearance, rather all the preparations are the preparatory for the purification of the hearts, as the purification of the hearts is the preparatory for their complement.

And the Shaykh Second Martyr said: there is in tradition that God won't look at your faces (appearance) rather He observed your hearts.[1]

Shortly, purifying from the unpurified and the filth is necessary and one should try to mortify to be purified while standing and praying before God.

---

[1] *Al-Tanbihat.*

But recite unto them with truth the tale of the two sons of Adam how, they offered each a sacrifice and it was accepted from the one of them and it was not accepted from the other (the one) said: I will surely kill thee. (The other) answered: Allah accepts only from those who ward off (evil).[1]

The purification is one of the conditions for accepting the prayer, and the inner purification that the purification of which is the moral's incomings, like proud, envoy, negligence and so on all are the conditions of the accepting to the knowledgeable people and also is the condition of the prayer of the inner ones and to the stage of the purification rate up to the end.

And one of the important behaviors that the avoid of which is necessary and the brethren should keep it in mind is that if they would hear a word from some scholars of the jurisprudents and the knowledgeable ones, if it sounds strange to them it does not mean that the uttered of the word has committed any sins, thus they blame the uttered to the injustice act and thought, it should not be so understood that if somebody refers to the words like love, liking or so on he is *Sufi* or like that, because swear to the Friend's soul that by those words they mean the Quranic commentary and traditions.

Think in this holy tradition quoted of Imam Sadiq (*a*) about the healthy heart, pay attention if there is anything but essential annihilation sacrificed avoid I-ness and selfishness which is the expression of the learned ones and refer to nothing else. Have thought about the *Shabaniyyah* invoking uttered by Ali (*a*) and his sons that is the ultimate goal of the spiritual wayfarers and the following supplication:

Oh God take all the worldly material from as to I pay attention merely on thee, me and lighten our eyes on Thyself as to the

---

[1] *Surah al-Anam*: 27.

heart's eyes tears the veils' light reaching the source of glory and greatness, and our souls would belong to thy great paradise, what is meant by "the great paradise?" If the reality of you had a glimpse of Him and fainted before thy Glory"

It is not but the "faint" in the tongue of infallible (*a*) if the manifestation which is in great praying "*samat*" is anything but the manifestations and the visions in their tongue! Whether it is on the tongue of Gnostic any words higher than this holy tradition which has been approved both by the Sunni and the Shiah alike:

"No servant of my servant ever approaches me, unless through the deeds which are valuable to me and I obliged one to perform it and the servant approaches me through the prayer "*nafilah*" as far as he attracts my attention and I like him. Then because I like him then I will be his ears by which he hears his eyes by which he sees, his tongue by which he talks, his hands by which he takes if he calls me I will answer him, if he asks me something I bestow him."[1]

Shortly, the evidence is more than that can be explained in this limited scope. And our intention by the words is that our brethren would approach them somehow to the mystical science and put aside their way of thinking toward the jurisprudents that uses such matters and are blamed as *Sufi* and so on. It is not for the sake of the jurisprudents being defended, rather for the main purpose because the value of man depends on his divine deeds not by whatever the others say about them we try to attract the readers attention to the divine knowledge and the inner purification that both of them are of the importance of the prophets' main duty and messages through their books oh dear, don't be tempted by Satan as to be contentment with whatever

---

[1] *Usul-e Kafi*, vol. 4, p. 53.

you possesses move a little and change yourself from the form without mind and the skin without lips, observe your behavior and your deeds and be acquainted with the utterance of the infallible (*a*) and the nobles' words in which there is blessing. Supposing you are acquainted with the theologians and jurisprudents follow some learned ones as all are Muslims, like Sayyid Ibn Tawus, Shaykh Jalil Bahai, Taqi Majlisi, Shaykh Muhaddithin, study some Persian books if you don't understand ask those who are knowledgably thereabout ask from the jurisprudents of the present time like Shaykh Javad Tabrizi perhaps you will effected by their words and don't waste your life like the writer of this book, because God forbid if you pass away with the some condition you will be much regretted and you can not make it up as the darkness is endless.

Oh God, wake up as from this heavy sleep and rescue us from I-ness and egoism and selfishness which is the source of all misleading and decayed and lead us to the straighten path, the path of humanity, God be the supporter for success

Chapter Two:

Some of the people of the knowledgeable say that the purification is either with water or with earth which is the vital mystery, that its origin is knowledge for the vision And he it is who sends the winds glad tiding her landing his mercy, and we send down purifying water from the sky.[1]

When you as a reassurance from Him and sent down water from the sky upon you, that thereby He might purify you, and remove from you the fear of Satan and made strong your hearts and firm (your) feet thereby or earth which is the origin of the human

---

[1] *Surah al-Furqan*: 49.

appearance: we were created from soil.[1] Oh ye! Who believe...and ye find out water, then go to high clean so if and rub your face and your hands therewith, O Allah is Benign forgiving[2]—depart unto the shadow falling three fold[3]. And this is for the reason by which you think about the created essence, then you become humble and avoid being proud, since the soil is the origin of indigence and base the writer says: the origin of water is: [Have not those who disbelieve known that heavens and the earth were of one piece, then we parted them and we made everything of water.[4]

And Imam Sadiq (*a*) says: "Approach water as you approach the God's Bounty"[5]

Imam Sadiq (*a*) Approach water as much as you approach the God's blessing.[6]

And that is the real divine manifestation without belonging to the appearances and the determinations within the one's verses. Then if the spiritual wayfarer finds a way to the manifestation of emanation and the unlimited feature as example to that manifestation of steps' purification of his own being as to achieve the union to the divine proximity, as the God's messenger (*a*) while performing abolition in ascension said: "Verily the earth is one the two cleaners"[7]

The secret of abolition is the removing of filth and the *tayamom*—ablution with soil—is the vision of oneness and the

---

[1] *Surah Ta Ha*: 55.
[2] *Surah an-Nisa*: 43.
[3] *Surah al-Anbiya*: 30.
[4] *Surah al-Anbiya*: 30.
[5] *Misbah ash-Shariah*, Section 10.
[6] *Misbah ash-Shariah*, ch. 10.
[7] Akhund Khorasani (*a*).

secret of the ablution is vision of the Almighty God and removing the otherness.

"He is the first and the last, and he is knower of everything"[1]

And the ablution is the vision of sacred essence: If are sent through a thread from sky into the earth you will be taken off upon the God.[2]

And shortly, to our impression the ablution is merely washing hands and face: I saw nothing except through which are within God[3]" It is within something else.[4]

And also ablution is purification with water and ablution is his vision within the article's mirror:

"Whatever of good befallen on thee it is from Allah, and whatever of ill befallen on thee it is from Thyself. We have sent thee (Muhammad) as a messenger unto mankind and Allah is sufficient as witness.[5]

And the abolition is the remover of the defeats: Allah there is no God save him. He gutter you all unto a day of Resurrection whereof there is no doubt, who is truer in statement than Allah.[6]

Chapter Three:

It is stated in *Misbah ash-Shariah* that Imam as-Sadiq (*a*) said: "When you intend purification and ritual ablution, proceed to the water as you proceed to Allah's mercy, because Allah has made water the key to His proximity and supplication, and a guide to

---

[1] *Surah Hadid*: 3.
[2] *Ilm al-Yaqin*, vol. 1, p. 34.
[3] *Ilm al-Yaqin*, vol. 1, p. 54.
[4] *Tawhid Saduq*, p. 36
[5] *Surah an-Nisa*: 79.
[6] *Surah an-Nisa*: 78.

the court of His service. And, as Allah's mercy purifies the sins of the servants, similarly the outer filths are purified by water and by nothing else." Allah, the Exalted, says: "And He it is who sends the winds as good news heralding His mercy, and We send down purifying water from the sky."[1] He also says: "And we made every living thing of water. Will they not then believe?"[2] So, as He has given life with water to everything of the blessings of this world, likewise, he has made obedience the life of the hearts, out of His mercy and grace. Think of the clarity, softness, purity and blessing of water and of its tender mixing with everything. Use it to purge the organs that Allah has ordered you to purify, and observe their disciplines in His obligations and advantages so, if you use them respectfully, the springs of the advantages will burst out for you presently. Then, mix with the creatures (servants) of Allah like the mixture of water with things: It gives to everything its due without any change in its own meaning. And learn a lesson from the Messenger of Allah (s) (who said): "A sincere believer is like water." Let your clearness with Allah, the Most High, be like the clearness of water as He sent it down from the sky and called it "purifier". Purify your heart with fear of Allah and certitude as you cleanse your organs with water.[3]

In these noble traditions there are delicate points and facts, which enliven the hearts of the people of knowledge, and bestow animation on the clear souls of "The people of heart".

Describing water, in this tradition as Allah's mercy, or interpreting it to be so, denotes that water is one of the great manifestations of Allah's mercy, which He sent down to the world of nature, and made it the source of life for the beings.

---

[1] *Surah al-Furqan* 25:48.
[2] *Surah al-Anbiya* 21:30.
[3] *Misbah ash-Shariah*, ch. 10, on "Purification".

Rather, the vast divine mercy, which descended from the high heaven of His Names and attributes, and with which the lands of the individual entities were revived, is called "water" by the people of knowledge. And as the vast divine mercy is more obvious in the apparent substance of water than in other things, Allah, the Exalted, has assigned to it the task of purifying the outer filths, and made it the key to the door of His proximity and of the supplications to him, and the guide to the court of his service, which is the door of the doors of the inner mercies. Actually, the water of Allah's mercy descends and appears in every growth of existence and in every visible and invisible scene to purify the sins of Allah's servants according to that growth and suitable to that world. So, the invisible sins of the individual entities are purified with the water of mercy which descends from the heaven of His Oneness, and the sins of the non-existence of "the outer nudities" are purged with the water of the vast mercy descending from the heaven of His Unity in every stage of existence according to that stage. In the stages of human growths, too, the water of mercy has different manifestations, as with the water descending from His Essence onto: "The purgatorial collective individuations" the sins of the "existential secret" is purified: "Your existence is a sin incomparable with any other sin." With the water descending from His Names and Attributes and the manifestation of Act, the vision of the attribute and the act is purged with the water descending from the sky of His "Decree of Justice" the inner moral impurities are purified. With the water descending from the sky of His Forgiveness the sins of the servants are purged. And with the water descending from the sky of "the kingdom of heaven" the formal impurities are purged. So, it is clear that Allah, the Exalted has made water the key to His proximity and the guide to His court of mercy. Then, in the noble tradition there is another instruction, which opens another way to the people of wayfarer and of observance. It says: "... Think of the clarity, softness, purity and blessing of water and of its tenderly mixing with everything. Use it to purge the organs, which Allah has ordered you to purify, and observe their disciplines in His obligations and traditions, as under each one there are many advantages. So, if you use them respectfully, the springs of the advantages will burst out for you presently. "

This noble tradition refers to the degrees of purity in general and puts it in four general degrees, of which one is that which is mentioned so far in the noble tradition, i.e. purifying the organs. It also notes that the people of observance and the *salik*s to Allah should not stop at the apparent form of the things. They have to regard the appearance as a mirror reflecting the inside, to detect the facts from the forms and not to be satisfied with formal purification, which is a satanic snare. So, in the purity of water they discover the purity of the organs, which they have to purge and clarify by way of performing the obligatory duties and the divine laws, whose fineness is to be used to make fine the organs and to take them out of the coarseness of disobedience, and to let purity and blessing flow into all the organs. And, from the tenderly mixing of water with things, they realize how the divine heavenly powers are mixed with the world of nature, preventing the impurities of nature from affecting them. When the organs are clothed with the divine obligations and laws and their disciplines, the inner advantages gradually appear, the springs of the divine secrets burst out and a part of the secrets of servitude and purity uncover themselves for the wayfarer. After explaining the first stage of purification and its instruction, the tradition gives the secondary instruction, saying: "... then mix with the creatures (servants) of Allah like the mixture of water with things: It gives to everything its due without any change in its own meaning. And learn a lesson from the Messenger of Allah (*s*) (who said): "A sincere believer is like water."

Think of the tendency of water and its mixture with some other things that mixture is for betterment and reform.

Chapter Four:
[On the secret of the holy tradition]

Imams (*a*) are quoted to have said: As Adam (*a*) was approaching to that tree and faces that tree as Adam (*a*) was absorbed in paradise and had no attention to the tree at all, and if he had remained in that absorption state he would have been out of humanity and would have never reached the circulation of perfection:

Adam went toward that tree hoping that he would remain in paradise for ever, for the joy of this he put it on his head, and then it was ordered that this limb should be cleaned as to purify the Adam's crime.[1]

Then the God Almighty's "Will" was accrued in such manner that the God's bounty should be expanded in this appearance, starts bestowing bounty and blessing and expels the jewel treasure of the realm of the world from the nature area and took out its valuable As to some of the infallible prophets and holy men [*awliya*] (*a*), they have no absolute[2] infallibility and are not protected against Satan's intrusion, such as Adam's act with respect to the "tree" which was one of the intrusions of the great Satan, the chief of the Satan, and despite the fact that the "tree" was a paradisiacal divine tree, yet it was marked by a multiplicity of names, which is contrary to the state of complete humanity. This is one of the meanings, or of the ranks, of "the forbidden tree".

---

[1] Shaykh Saduq, *Majlis* 35.
[2] *The Discipline of the Prayer*, Imam Khomeini, p. 46.

If the light of the divine disposition was polluted with the formal and spiritual impurities, it would be at a distance from the court of the Proximity and "the Presence of love" in proportion to its pollution, until the light of disposition completely goes outside, secret and open, are put at the disposal of Satan. Thus, Satan becomes its heart, ear (hearing) eye (seeing), hand, and leg, and all his other organs become Satanic. If somebody absolutely wretched and will never see the face of happiness. And it was impossible unless by Adam's attention to the nature and coming out from unconsciousness into the sobriety state and out of the God's abortion and leaving the paradise, therefore made the inner power to overcome him and the outer Satan, invited him to approach this tree the sacred of the expansion of the perfections and the main conquering of the doors of blessings. Thus he was exiled from the divine proximity before falling he was invited to the nature as to enter the veil of darkness, because unless he enters the veils of darkness it would not be torn. Said God Almighty: We have created human then we returned him to the utmost corner, the worst, the lowest place the worst place which is the last veil of darkness is the surprising and is the needed names and attributes.

And when Adam (*a*) by the heaven appearance was expelled to its own dominion and committed a great sin. And when such attention in the stage or the worldly paradise has been found expression, the world changed into a tree and seemed like a tree Adam was attracted and went toward it took it by hands and put it on his head, he committed sin. After having committed this sin and being polluted with it caused these people [of today] repay for his fault.

Then, the filth appeared and then he had to remove and clean the mess and also the offspring's, too have to clean the mess, especially these people who are the Gnostic of the secrets have to compensate. The apparent pollution should be purified through the sent down water [rain] and the inner pollution and the heart's pollution through the manifestation of divine stage. Then while purifying the place, the heart should be purified by moving and removing the otherness thoroughly, and while purifying hands, from the elbow up to the end of the fingers, then watering the head while forgetting the world and the all the worldly articles and coming out of the committed sin by the first father.

Then God Almighty said: "Oh Muhammad bring forth your hand as to be washed through the water which is pouring from my sky." Then water poured and I touched it, so the beginning of abolition was started in this way by the right hand then he said: Muhammad take that wash your face, and the way of washing was taught to that holy man, because you want to look at the glory, you must be clean then go to the left side and follow suite, and with the rest of that water wash the other limbs, foot...the tradition is continued.[1]

You, too, oh the sincere learned friend, and brethren, you follow suit and intimate the head of leader of the Gnostic people and the faithful ones. Stretch your right hand toward God's blessing and gain from the poured water behalf of the God, as the God won't deprive the poor and won't send them back empty handed thus rake some of those blessed water and purify yourself.[2] So, it must be noted that as the external form of the prayer is not proved to be correct without the purity of the clothes and the body, and as impurities—which are of Satan's vile acts and cause repellence from the presence of the Beneficent—block the way of attending the Presence, the prayer's place with clothes and body polluted with Satan's vileness is expelled from the divine presence and prevented from attending the station of

---

[1] *Ilal ash-Sharai*, p. 312.
[2] *The Discipline of the Prayer*, Imam Khomeini, p. 48.

familiarity. Similar is the vileness of disobeying Allah, which is also of Satan's practices and of the filths of that foul creature. It also prevents one from entering the presence. So, the red-handed disobedient one, with an impure cover of the isthmus this cover is among the conditions for the realization and correctness of the internal prayers. As long as man is in the veil of this world, he cannot know about the invisible body, the purity and filth of its clothes and the condition of its being pure and without filth. The day he comes out of this veil, and the sovereignty of the interior and of the day of gathering twists aside the extensive disunion of the exterior, and the eye of the invisible interior opens, and the eye of the visible animalist closes, thereupon, with the eye of insight, he will understand that his prayers, had been, till the end of life, void of purity and surrounded by thousands of obstacles, each one of which was an independent cause for expelling one from the Holy presence of Allah. Alas! A thousands alas! The worlds are the two rival wives. So much your hand from the above elbow up to the end of the fingers with this intention "There is no movement, no power but God". Because with such filthy soul one can not touch the God's Book: and through its blessing, while washing your head removing the proud and selfishness as to gain the God's bounty, and purify as to be the intimate of the proximity stage and step forward as to be deserve to the God's court. There will be nothing but regret and remorse-endless regrets and continuous remorse: "And warn them of the day of anguish when the matter shall have been decided..."[1]

After that the clothes of the interior body became pure, it would be necessary for the very invisible body to be purified from Satan's filth, that is, purification from the filths of the dispraised characters, as each one of them is apt to pollute the interior and to expel man from the presence and prevent him from the

---

[1] *Surah Maryam* 19:39.

proximity. Such characters are of the filths of Satan who is deprived of (Allah's) mercy. The origins of all the dispraised acts are self-conceit, selfishness, ostentation, and obstinacy, each of which are the origin of many dispraised characters, and is at the head of many sins.

Having completed this purification, and purified the clothes of *Raqwa* with the water of sincere repentance and lawful austerity, the *salik* will have to busy himself with the purification of the heart, which is the real concealed, and into which Satan's intrusion is greater, and its impurities spread to other clothes and conceivers. So, without purifying the heart passes through several stages, some of which will be referred to in these pages.

One of them is purging the heart from loving this world, which is at the head of all sins and it is the origin of all corruptions. As long as man has this love in his heart, it will not be possible for him to be admitted to the presence of Allah.

And, if you recall Allah sincerely and in reality and if you comprehend the reality of the name and the named through the teachings of teaching names you will be subjected the address; *"dhakarani abdi"* otherwise you will be refused or *"kadhibite hadiani"*, thus be quite and wait for the address *"ahamdani"* of Allah. Then focus the entire praising sincerely and heartily upon the God as to be subjected the address *"hamadani abdi"* otherwise consider yourself to be addressed *"ya munafiq"*. And if you call God through the blessing mercifulness and benevolence you will be honored with *"athni ala abdi"* and when you say *"maliki yawmid-din wa iyyaka nabudu wa iyyaka nastain"* you wait for the *"majadani abdi"* and then be ready for expelling from the limitation, the present address from them invisible determination, rather the veil of names and attributes: "You do we worship and you do we seek help from" takes place in that particular privacy and the meeting familiarity, for this reason he said: "This is between me and my servant" And when the everlasting favor encompasses him and awakens him, he will demand consistency of this stage and establishment of His presence, by requesting, guide us to the straight path," in which "Guide us" is interpreted to mean: "Make us firm, consistent and steady." This is for those who have slipped out of the veil and attained "the eternally wanted" as to us the people of the veil; we will have to ask Allah, the exalted, for guidance with its ordinary concept.

The writer says: And also as far as the spiritual wayfarer is within the shape of obedience all his rituals and prayers are from the servant, and when he is effaced in Allah all his deeds namely praising is through God's aspect, he has no any role in it. And when the sobriety after-self-effacement occurred Allah is servant and servant has no any role, it does not mean the servant ceases worshipping, no rather he must worship: "And would be his eyes, his tongue, and his ears,[1] and whatever the ignorant of *Sufi* have taught is defect and when the servant becomes sobriety, the worship belongs to God: The servant is God's tongue and God's ears.

Chapter Five:
[The secrets of the nakedness]

And to the ordinary people is the covering of all his internal and external vices of the body in the presence of Allah of nakedness in order to observe the presence and the discipline of presence.

And by the people of the faith is the covering of the vices of hearts by the clothes of trust, and to the people of the knowledge and discover the covering of vices is the covering of the secret by the clothing of vision. And to the people of guardianship

---

[1] *Usul-e Kafi*, vol. 4, p. 53.

infallible the covering of vices is the secret of the secret by the clothing of obeying. In short when the spiritual wayfarer finds himself in all aspects—affairs state—being the very presence he covers all his internal and external kinds of nakedness in order to observe the presence and discipline of presence. And the God Almighty, the great generous and vast coverer, is the coverer of all the vices of the creatures through his mercy covered this human by different clothing as to cover them from the apparent vices of the body. And covered the vices misdeed by the heaven veil, and such covering veil had not been over our creatures' misdeeds and the hidden parts of them would be visible we would have been disgraced and degraded in this world, but God almighty and lofty through his covering hid these deeds from being seeing by the others and covered the ethical vices and kept them and if had shown the real deeds and the real forms as it has been in reality:

Some people will be appeared in such faces that comparing with them the monkeys and the parks are beautiful.[1]

And in tradition *Kafi*[2] it has been quoted of the reliable: "The proud will be appeared in the form of a weak ant and people will put their foot on this head, as to be served out by the people."

Shortly, in this case the human form is the Allah's covering veil which has been covered upon our inner nakedness, as he covered the vices of the hearts and secrets through the essential, nominal and agent covering and it goes to all heavenly and worldly creatures according to their stages.

It must be noted that if he does not cover himself with Allah's veiling and forgiveness and if he does put himself under the Names of "The concealed " and the "forgiver" demanding

---

[1] *Ilm al-Yaqin*, vol. 2, p. 901.
[2] *Usul-e Kafi*, vol. 3, p. 424.

concealment and forgiveness it frequently happens that when the visible curtain is rolled up, and the worldly veil is removed, they cause his exposure in the presence of the favorable angels and the appointed prophets (*a*) Allah alone knows how much the exposed internal nakedness is ugly, disgraceful, stinking and scandalous.

Connection: It is stated in *Misbah ash-Shariah* that Imam as-Sadiq (*a*) said: "The most decorative clothing for the believer is the clothing *taqwa*, and the finest one is faith. Allah, the Almighty and glorified, said: "And the clothing of *taqwa*, that is the best." As to the exterior clothing, it is a blessing from Allah, as it covers the nakedness of the children of Adam (*a*). It is a grace granted to other than them. To the believers, it is a means to perform the duties imposed by Allah upon them. The best of your clothing is that which does not distract you from Allah, the Almighty and glorified, rather it brings you nearer to thanking, remembering and obeying Him, and it does not bear you to conceit, hypocrisy, decoration, taking pride and boasting, as these are among the pests of the religion and bring cruelty to the heart. When you put on your dress, remember Allah, the concealer of your sins by His mercy. Clothe your interior with truthfulness, as you dressed your exterior with your dress. Let your interior be under the protection of fear, and your exterior under the protection of obedience. Take a lesson from the favor of Allah, the Almighty and Glorified, as He created the means for making clothes to conceal the apparent nakedness, and He opened the doors of repentance and imploring in order to cover the internal sins and evil characters. Do not uncover anyone's faults, as Allah has covered your greater faults. Attend to your own faults, and forgive that whose state and affairs do not concern you. Beware of perishing your life for the action of others, letting the others trade with your capital, while you destroy yourself. Forgetting the sins is of the gravest punishments from Allah in this world, and of the most effective causes for the punishments in the Hereafter. As long as the servant is engaged in his obedience to Allah, the Exalted, in recognizing his own defects and abandoning what is disgraceful in the religion of Allah, he will be isolated from the plagues, plunging in the sea of the mercy of Allah, the Almighty and glorified, and will win the gems of the advantages of wisdom and expression. But as long as he is forgetting his sins, unfamiliar with his defects, resorting to his own might and force, he will never be successful."

Think and cogitate about this comprehensive word for the people of learned and the followers of the hearts will reveal the doors of knowledge and show the quality of dealing between the servants and God.

The spiritual wayfarer should always remember God Almighty and never neglects Him, he must always observes servitude and the stage of Lordship almighty, even in social and ordinary affairs, he must observe the heart's and the soul's manners and remembers the God's blessing in the shape of whatever he sees. Thus while the spiritual wayfarer wearing the apparent cloth through the faith and knowledge origin, which are the best clothes he should not forget God.

Thus in covering the appearance, he must close that sort of clothes suitable and respectable, not the suite and clothes which cause him neglect God Almighty and put him within the circle of the proud people. He must know such behaviors are so effective which may bring the spiritual wayfarer on the threshold of perdition, and he should know such bad case which occurred through the luxury clothes is the disease of the heart, namely the source of all corruptions.

While wearing clothes, recalling God and his blessing internally and externally which have been totted to him and deed with sincerely, and cover apparent with clothes and the inner part with fear and respect to and recall the God's grace which cause him had cover internal and externally and said to repent, and opened the way of repenting to his servants that through his covering covers the defects and the sins.

And as the God is the coverer of his servants, he likes the coverers and hates those who reveal the defects of the others. Thus, the spiritual wayfarer, two is the coverer of the God's servants and he does not waste to reveal the others' veil of honor as the God has covered his faults so he should be careful not to reveal anybody's veil, and secret because God uncovers his misdeeds and makes him scandal and defame and abase.

And the spiritual wayfarer had better pay attention on finding his own faults, rather than the others' faults searching and spending his time on the affairs which is useless for him ever it harms his as well, the spiritual way farer doesn't consider his own deeds the best of all through gossiping and unveiling the secrets A wayfarer should never forget his own sins and faults because forgetting sins the worst and biggest misdeeds bring a heavy punishment in hereafter.

And as far as the God's creature is busy praising God and searching his own faults and he is away from whatever is forbidden he is saved from calamities and is given numerous bounty and if he forgets his own sins and neglects his faults and becomes selfish and I-ness and relied upon himself, he won't be prosperous and won't achieve victory.

Chapter six:
Some cordial disciplines for removing filth and purifying impurities

Impurity (filth) is to eschew from the proximity stage and being veiled and covered from the sacred stage. It is against and opposite to the union of devotee and the proximity of the nobles' spirits.

And that to the ordinary people is the ordinary impurity and to the singled out ones spiritual impurity and to the learned and the knowledgeable and the follower of the hearts all the world, to the separation aspect which is the manifestation of Satan and there is on the privacy discipline: "I seek protection from God against the dirty Satan, the dirty and filthy maker, being expelled from the God's court.[1]

And said God: "Avoid the dirt."[2]

Thus, whatever is different with the proximity stage, to the beloved's proximity, make away from you and try to avoid it. Keep away from the apparent filth by cleaning the body. But removing the external filth and impurities has no such position, because it is a superficial cleaning and an external purification. Its cordial discipline is that the wayfarer servant, who wants to be present in the presence of Allah, is to know that with satanic filth and impurity one cannot find his way there, and unless he comes out from the big moral dispraised acts, which are the source of the corruption of the human utopia and the origin of the external and internal sins, he will have no way to wanted the goal.

---

[1] *Wasail ash-Shiah*, vol. 1, p. 217.
[2] *Surah al-Muddaththir*: 5

Whose migrates for the cause of Allah will find much refuge and who's for sakes his home fugitive unto Allah and his messengers, and death overtakes him, his reward is then liniment on Allah?[1]

Then it was obvious that this spiritual journey and the proximity ascension, possesses two aspects, the former resulted from the purifying the secret of which is evacuating and the main aspect of which is derived from prayer that the secret of which is purification of "*tawhid*:" "Take away the lamp as the sun is rising"[2]

And if the life permits the divine Gnostic he is able to go through the whole course of ascension, from the beginning till the ultimate goal, expel it from this divine mixture and the connection between the servant and the creator. But this debate is out of our scope of our discussion.

Chapter Seven:
[About knowing the place]

And to the all people is known and the condition of which in the theologian books have been written. And by the jurisprudent ones are all the world and "*musala*" is the entire creature. And in "secret of reading" will be discussed about –God willing-that the whole world is praising the God Almighty and all are humble before Him. And here it should be known that the obedience heaven is the temple of all creatures and all creatures are busy praising God- the inner part of each particle you discover a sun you will be see inside. It is due to the God's nature's light that they are invited to the perfect modesty:

---

[1] *Surah an-Nisa*: 100.
[2] *Majalis al-Muminin*, vol. 2, p. 11.

The seven heavens and earth and all that is there in praise him, and there is not a thing but hymneth his praise, but ye understand not their praise. Lo! He is ever clement forgiving.[1]

And to the infallible (*a*) it is the entire heaven's limitation and the agent of the temple of the mighty God and "*Musala*" is the very essence of the God Almighty. And to the people of guardianship. The whole agent and nominal determinations is the God's temple and *Musala* is the God's essence. Then in nominal and attributable determinations *Musala* is right and its prayer's place the soul of determination and the great name: "No praising I can praise Thee, Thou art what Thou Art, as Thou praised Thyself."[2]

And in agent manifestation through the sacred emanation *Musala* is the determination of world and the God Almighty is *Musala* in this agent manifestation: "Verily Thy God prays and says: pure and sacred is God of angel and spirit.[3]

Thus, the world's determination within the presence manifestation and the dissension curve the God's temple and the God Almighty is the Beloved, and in the absent manifestation and the ascension curve the temple of the creature and the visible Beloved.

Connection: It is stated in *Misbah ash-Shariah* that Imam as-Sadiq (*a*) said: "When you arrive at the door of the mosque, know that you have come to the door of a great King. No one may walk into his courtyard but the truthful. So, attach reverence to your coming to the ground of serving the King, as you would be exposed to a great danger if you were negligent. Know that he is capable of doing what he likes of justice and grace with you

---

[1] *Surah al-Isra*: 44.
[2] *Misbah ash-Shariah*, ch. 5, p. 381.
[3] *Usul al-Kafi*, vol. 2, p. 329.

and by you. So, if he were kind to you with his mercy and favor, he would accept from you little worship and give you much reward for it. But if he demanded from you a share of truth and sincerity, to be just with you, he is the doer of what he wants. Confess to His presence your inability, shortcoming, humility and poverty, as you have come to Him to worship and to get His intimacy. Expose your secrets to Him, knowing that nothing, covert and overt, of the entire universe, is hidden from Him. Before Him, be the poorest of His servants. Empty your heart of all occupants that keep you away from your Lord, as He does not accept except the pure(sty) and the (most) sincere. Find out in which register your name is recorded. If you tasted the sweetness of supplication and the delight of addressing Him, and drank from the cup of His mercy and generosity out of His good reception of you and response to you, then you would become suitable for His service. So, enter, as you will have permission and protection. Otherwise, stop, like the one whose rope has snapped, whose hope has come short, and time has got the better of him. So, if Allah found in your heart true recourse to Him, He would look at you with the eye of kindness, mercy and leniency, and cause you to be successful in attaining what he likes and is pleased with, since He is generous and loves generosity for His servants who distressfully resort to Him and burn out at His door for the want of His pleasure. Allah, the most high, says: "Or, who answers the distressed one, when he calls upon Him, and removes the evil?"

I have related the complete text of this noble speech because it is a comprehensive set of instructions for the people of knowledge and the wayfarers to Allah, who, by contemplating on it may acquire a different state.

And when the people of divine knowledge observe scholar of the mosque is the Lordship must be careful enter the mosque purified externally and internally, as in the sacred place the filthy ones are not allowed to enter and only the devotee and the purified are allowed to enter the mosque. Thus in all cases the feel danger and are threatened by the great risk because of being negligence at the divine court are frightened and their hearts are trembling because of the one served out according to their deeds and behaviors and they will be asked for purity and sincerity and then they will be expelled from the proximity court. Thus, confessing to the guilt, sin and fault and being indigence and poor and release and free their own hearts from the multiple affairs which make them away and keep them aside from the God's attention, as the know they can approach in this course only through sincere and purified heart and all. And as this stage has been achieved and all tendencies have been put aside, the children and other affairs went out of the mind and makes room for the love of God, they will enjoy the sweetness of praying and worshipping and will be toxicities through the unique love to the real beloved. They deserve being entered to the proximity court then by the permission and allowance of God within the area of the world which is the Lordship's mosque step in and such deed is lawful.

And those who are not able to achieve such stage and permission are the trespassers of the God's abode and the unjust to the God's house. Then they have to keep in trying to shorten their desires and for this appeal to God and say:

"It is not He (best) who answers the wrong one when he cries unto Him and removes the evil and has made you victory of the earth? Is there any God beside Allah? Little do they reflect!"[1]

And when the God Almighty observes their true sayings he will compensate their defect through His mercy and will announce his satisfaction: He is generous and loves generosity for his

---

[1] *Surah an-Naml*: 62.

servants who distressfully resort to Him and burn out at his door.[1]

Chapter Eight:
[On some disciplines concerning permissibility of place]

And that the special jurisprudents releasing from the Satan's domination and avoid disobeying God's limitations. And to the knowledgeable people and the Gnostic ones, exiting from the domination of desire through the lack of seeing ones own authority. And to the infallible departure from the absolute domination in essence and names and attributes.

And as much as the limbs and hearts remain under Satan's control or the desire's control the God's temple and the soldiers' of Allah are usurping and the God's worship won't take place therein and will the worships are for Satan and the desire. And having cut the intruding hand of Satan short off the kingdom of the heart which is the private residence of Allah, and purified his heart for Allah's manifestation and excluded otherness than Allah such as evil from it the external and the internal mosques and the visible places and invisible places permissible for him, and his prayer become like those of the people of knowledge and consequently the purity of the mosque is realized too: and he will give you another, blessing which you love: help from Allah and present victory (the rank-b) .And the description of which is out of the scope of these pages.

---

[1] *Misbah ash-Shariah*, Section 12.

Chapter Nine:
[On the secrets of the time]

And in the conducts of the learned ones and the manner of the people of the faith, from the down till the ultimate rising which is noon that is the time for God's praying and the Prophet's (*a*) prayer peace be upon him and his Household (*a*) in ascension which is the lighting manifestation: the beneficent one, who is established on the throne.[1]

And from this, the secret of its occurrence in ascension will be found out. Though the ascension occurred at night and lasted up to dawn: And serve Thy Lord till the Inevitable [death] comes unto thee.[2]

Thus from the starting of noon time which shortens the day time: Hast thou not seen how thy Lord Hath spread the shade and if he will have made the sun its pilot.[3]

Up to the time that under the horizon it sets down: the time of the evening prayers which are the main prayers: And when the sun reaches its end the two times (noon and the evening) have arrived (for praying).[4]

Though to the Gnostic's conduct both are prayers up to the primarily and the secondary: verily those four parts are instead of another four.[5]

And in traditions both have been called "Prayers" And the time for the afternoon prayer is the time of Adam's sin entering into the veil of tendency toward the nature tree. But the time for the

---

[1] *Surah Ta Ha*: 5.
[2] *Surah al-Hijr*: 99.
[3] *Surah al-Furqan*: 45).
[4] *Man la yahduruhu al-faqih*, tradition 3.
[5] *Wasail ash-Shiah*, vol. 3, p. 211.

evening prayer is in the time of the darkening world and the entire vanishing of the real sun. There is a tradition has been quoted of the infallible (*a*): the evening is when that the Adam repented then he observed prayer—three parts—one for himself, second one for the Eve sin and the third one for his own repentance. And the *isha* prayer is for the time when the grave and the resurrection day is dark. This darkness will be removed by such prayer and the bridge will be illuminated for them.

But the morning prayer is from the very beginning of light—dawn—up to the time before rising the sun in another word, by the tongue of the Gnostic ones from the beginning of vanishing the darkness and appearing the real light: "Establish worship at the going down of the sun until the dark of night and—the recital of—the Quran at dawn. Lo!—the recital of-the Quran at dawn is ever witnessed.[1]

And the time of the Morning Prayer which is the God's necessary duty is the time of overcoming the day over night: establish worship.[2]

And after sunrise: It has come to its end. Then the whole sacred Muhammadi Night is the whole circle of being, if you appreciate, and it is the resurrection Ahmadi Day if you stand for giving service.

Connection:
[On watching over the time]

Be aware that the watching the time of the prayers' time namely having the date for being present at the Lord's presence, is considered so important to the careful devotees as the faithful of worshiping and conducts wait for such moments and prepare

---

[1] *Surah al-Isra*: 78.
[2] *Surah al-Isra*: 78.

themselves and their hearts for entering therein and while being purified internally and externally go toward it and leave aside all other affairs, forget the worldly business make their heart completely cut from the otherness and think merely to the meeting place of God. Some wives of the Messenger of Allah (*s*) were quoted to have said: "The Messenger of Allah (*s*) used to talk to us and we used to talk to him. But when the time for the prayers arrived he appeared as if he did not know us and we did not know him, as his attention was completely directed to Allah." It is said that Amir al-Muminin Ali (*a*), when it was time for the prayers, used to writhe and tremble. Asked once about his uncommon state, he said: "The time has come for the trust which Allah, the Exalted, offered to the heavens and the earth and the mountains, but they refused to carry it and were afraid of it." Sayyid Ibn Tawus (may his soul be sanctified) says in *Falah as-Sail*, that when Imam Husayn (*a*) used to perform the *wudu*, he changed colors and his joints trembled. Asked about the reason, the Imam said: "When one is going to stand before the Owner of the Arsh, his color is ought to turn pale and his joints to tremble." Imam Hasan had a similar condition. It is narrated that Imam as-Sajjad (the fourth Imam) (*a*) used to get pale at the arrival of the time of the *wudu*. He was once asked: "What is this state which happens to you whenever you want to perform the *wudu*?" He said: "Do you not know before whose presence I am to stand?"

And there is in tradition that sitting in the mosque for waiting to pray itself is considered worship.[1]

Shortly, those who did not know the intercourse, worship and praise with the absolute Beloved and did not care for it, if they had been of the love and liking people they would have changed the eagerness and the pleasure of worshipping Allah to the world

---

[1] *Bihar al-Anwar*, vol. 3, p. 85.

of being and they would have kept themselves busy with the God's love and his worship, and if they were the people of the faith the faithful ones they would realize that the hereafter's life and the investment of which is worship of Allah and its physical paradise and its nymph and its castles confined in the frame of the human deeds: is effective only when one perform it thoughtfully deeply coupled with the presence of heart.

One of the factors which cause the perfect presence of heart is watching time and being punctual for prayer before God Almighty. And the spiritual wayfarer enabling to devout all his time to God at least five times of his time daily should be especially reserved for praising and worshipping, to meet God. One should appreciate God for such opportunity given to him to praise at the God's court and entering the proximity session. Thus the punctuality and dating with God which seems at first unimportant, it will be changed into: "And whoso doeth ill an atom's weight will see it then.[1]

After having realized the outcome and the importance of its deeds than should take care about the time thereabout. And we mentioned before about it that one of great secret of praising is that each one has its own effect and form on the heart which causes it illuminate and make the heart humble to the creator and brings forth perfect obedience for the soldiers of soul to the spirituality.

Thus the souls will be independent and each one of these affairs is important that is effective in the unseen realm. And the outcome of which is the sincere paradise which is above the deeds' paradise this affection upon the pray an important and principal reality quite meaningful. This helps praising pleasant and the spiritual wayfarer will find out the reality secret of the

---

[1] *Surah Zilzal*: 8.

praying which is the main gate of heart's and soul's worshipping and little by little the God's soldiers within the realm of one's essence watches praying and worshipping and it will be a discovery of praising features and glory upon the heart and achieves the first manifestation of *tawhid*. Afterwards the conduct's divine way will be opened for him and he will be deserved entering the real prayer by the help of God.

The Second Text

Chapter One:
[General secrets and disciplines of the *adhan* and *iqamah*]

Adhan to the distinguished people is the announcement of visible and invisible powers within the grownup and non grownup spirits preparing themselves for the *salat* announcing the presence by saying: Come to *salat hayya ala-s-salat*, twice. As to be present at the court of Allah, Almighty. Thus, with this primary *"takbir"*—calling God great—[In this stage] the discipline of the *salik* is to tell his heart and powers, even the innermost of the heart, that the time of presence is near so as to prepare for himself for that, fully observing the formal and the spiritual secret and result of the *salat* by the calling *hayya ala-s-salat*].

Its general discipline is to be aware of the greatness of the position, its significance and the majesty of the presence and present and it is servility helplessness, poverty, in capability, and shortcoming of the possible [existence] in carrying out orders and deserving to attend the meeting, unless the kindness and, mercy of Allah, the most high, extend the helping hand to make up for the shortcomings. And through the refusing essential divinity and the agent divinity due to the others but God and confined it within the sacred essence, refusing the praising and compliments to the others and the testimony to the prophet hood of the last messenger in absence and presence should appeal to the sacred essence absolute intersession that though the intercourse to that sacred essence which is the guardianship, such divine conducts will be through by him and to the union ascension will be exalted. And our perfect mystic Shaykh said: "Testimony to the God's guardianship is the in testimony to the prophethood because the guardianship is the inner nature of prophethood." Thus the sacred guardianship too, is the companion of this conduct. And in tradition: "Through Ali (*a*) set up the prayer, and by the tradition "I am the prayer and the fasting of the pious."

Thus, the spiritual wayfarer when announces his praising to the God Almighty: "First the companion then the way" announcing for the prayer: "*hayya ala-s-salat*" and he reads through the visible and invisible powers, then he announces the secret of the prayer concisely, namely he says: "*hayya ala al-falah, hayya ala khayr al-amal*" And he makes aware the human the soldiers both worldly and heavenly inviting them for demanding love of freedom and perfectionism that the both are of the divine nature and the whole men have been born with them. After having awakening the nature and preparing for the act, repeat *takbir* and worshipping God (by saying: there is no god but God) confessing weakness and being guilty as to be placed within the heart and the first and the last secrets will be appeared. And in *iqamah* he should purify the rows and prepares the soldiers internally and externally and keeps on repeating as to achieve the result. Trust the previous realities and ties firm the connection of appealing and makes aware the nature. And when the servant reaches this point by saying. "*Fa qad qamat as-salat*" announces his readiness.[1]

Thus, the spiritual wayfarer and the fighter on God's way should concentrate on heart and pay attention upon some other scattered powers, gather them together and the angles of heaven's inhabitants, and the scattered soldiers in different realms in the external through the heart, would gather together and the angels of the heavens will gather round him and follow him. And when the spiritual wayfarer found himself follow by the angels at the sacred presence, he should take care of his "*salat*" and avoid neglecting and mistaking: The pious by himself is congregation.[2] And if he looks after this congregation according to each pious he gains blessing and perhaps through the Allah's help gains some secrets: "*Iyyaka nabudu wa iyyaka nastain.*" Which is revealed to him? And if he does not care and some wrongs would happen in such process, he will be considered one of the hypocrites. He not only has spoiled his own *salat*, rather has spoiled the followers' angels, because "Imam" is responsible for his followers more over he is the carrier of the marginal conditions thereabout.

And the better and near way to rescue that his *musalli* gives it to spiritual Prophet (*a*) altogether or gives it to Imam of the era (*a*) and praises Allah through their tongue and appeal to them for his deeds and he himself who is the angel's and divine soldiers' Imam, changes into the follower of "*Wilayah*" and through such

---

[1] This, in itself, is one of the general affairs of the conduct and of the comprehensive disciplines concerning praising and worshipping, which must be before the *salik*'s eyes during the whole period of performing the prayers. That is why the calling God in the minds and the preliminary wording before entering the prayer, as well as in the prayer. It is also repeated when passing from one stage to another so that wayfarer's innate inability, and the Greatness and the Glory of the Sacred Essence are confirmed in his heart.

[2] *Wasail ash-Shariah*, vol. 5, p. 379.

spiritual conducts ascends to divine ascension through their lead, and would be a sincere and obeyed follower as the Ali (*a*) is the straight way and the pious' prayers and the Ilyas of the leading conducts: Don't step on this way without being led by Iliyas"

There is a reference to some of what has been said in a lengthy tradition in *Ilal ash-Shariah*, quoting Imam Jafar as-Sadiq (*a*) describing the ascending He said: "Allah, the Glorified and Almighty, sent down to the Prophet a carriage of light comprised of forty sorts of light which were around the heaven the heaven of Allah, Blessed and Most High, blurs the eyes of the onlookers. One of them was yellow, and it became the cause of the yellowness of the yellow. Another one was red, and it became the cause of the redness of the red…" Then, he added: "… He [the Messenger (*s*)] sat in it and it ascended him to the lower heaven. The angels ran to the outskirts of the heaven, and then they fell in prostration, and said: "All-glorified and All-holy is our Lord, the Lord of the angels and the Spirit. How this light is like the light of our Lord!" Jibrail (Gabriel) said: "God is great!" The angels stopped talking, and the heaven was opened. The angels gathered and came to pay tribute to the Prophet (*s*) group after group…" as the tradition goes.[1]

Then he said: ascending to the second heaven being seen by the angels fled around the heaven and genuflected and said: "How similar is this light to the light of our creator" Then Jibrail said: "*Ashhadu an la ilaha illallah*" twice.

Then he ascended to the second heaven, namely when the messenger of Allah (*s*) maintained on the mount of light and ascended accompanied by Gabriel and reached the second heaven, the angels ran away, bowed and glorified Allah, Gabriel said": I testify that Muhammad is the Messenger of Allah. I

---

[1] *Ilal ash-Shariah*, vol. 2, p. 312, sec. on "The causes of the *wudu*, the *adhan* and the *Salat*, *hadith* 1, p. 312.

testify that Muhammad is the messenger of Allah, the angles gathered and greeted the messenger of Allah, and asked him about Amir al-Muminin (Ali), the doors of the heavens opened and the messenger ascended to the fourth heaven. There, the angels of Allah said nothing. Then the door of the heaven opened and the angels gathered, and Gabriel finished reciting the *iqamah*.

There are some secrets and realities in this tradition beyond the access and out reach and whatever we comprehend from which through our small brain if we mention it will be a long story and out of the scope of these pages. And by mentioning some points of it, was to show the *iqamah* of the angels. Muhammad Moslem said: when you recite the *iqamah* and *iqamah*, two rows of angels will perform the *salat* behind you, but if you said the *iqamah* only one row of the angels would perform the *salat* behind you. There are many other traditions to the same effect, some of which say that the length of each row is the distance between the east and the west, and the length of the shortest is between the heaven and the earth. The difference among the narratives may be due to the difference among the knowledge and sincerity of the *musallin* and their prayers.[1]

In this noble tradition there are great secrets to which the hand of our hopes is too short to reach, and what can be said is now out of our purpose, like the secret of the secret of their diversity, the secret of their gathering around the heaven, the truth of the heaven in this respect, the secret of the yellowness of the yellow and the redness of the red caused by them, the secret of the angels' running, their bowing, praising and glorifying, and likening his light to Allah's and the like. To speak about each of them would be lengthy. Yet, that which suits this occasion and testifies to our subject is that the angels of Allah quieted down as

---

[1] *Wasail ash-Shariah*, vol. 4, p. 620.

they heard Gabriel's God is great, and gathered around the candle of the meeting of the Absolute Guardian. By that God is great the first heaven opened, and one of the curtains, which blocked the way to Allah, was drawn away. It should be noted that the curtains, which are pushed aside by the *adhan* are other than the curtains, which are in the opening. We shall probably refer to this concept later on, Allah willing.

Concerning there being only two God is great in the *iqamah*, it is probably because the wayfarer has set up his powers in the Presence, and has somewhat advanced from multiplicity toward unity, magnifying the Essence and the Names, or the Names and the Attributes; and it may be that the magnification of the Essence and the Names implies the magnification of the Attributes and the Acts.

Chapter Two:
[On the secrets of *qiyam*]

And to the noble ones, "*iqamah*" is stability at the presence of the sacred God and hurriedness for obeying and expelling out of covering and standing upon awareness: O thou enveloped in thy cloak. Thy raiment purifies.[1] And residence in manner and justice in behaviors, and disliking two extremes as there is in Rizam tradition. Mawla Khalid Abdullah which has been referred to in the previous pages, Imam Sadiq (*a*) about the reality of the prayer said: Being bold for the enemy is needed but to be kind and humble before the friends. Abraham was neither a Jew, nor yet Christian, but he was an upright man who had surrounded to Allah and there is in tradition that the messenger (*a*) drew a straight line and drew some line around it and said:

---

[1] *Surah al-Muddaththir*: 1-4.

"This straight line is my own way." It has been said that he said: "The verse had made me old."[1]

This is referred to: "So tread thou straight path as thou art commanded and those who turn (unto Allah) with thee, and transgress not. Lo: He is seer of what ye do.[2] And our perfect learned Shaykh, Shah Abadr, used to say: "This utterance is due to this reason that he is asked for being confirm as if he were the followers. Therefore the same verse has come in the holy *Surah ash-Shawra*: Unto this, then, summon (O' Muhammad).[3]

And he did not mention for that case because it is lack of that continuation.

Shortly, residence and avoid exiting from the midlines in all stages is above all the affairs for the spiritual wayfarer which should be while being in *"Qiyam"* state standing before Allah due to the lack of standing for orders as it should be, being ashamed and bows his neck for being repentance and regretted and focuses his eyes upon the earth for being ashamed and confesses his own guilt and admit his being weak, poor and sinful and finds himself at the presence of the God Almighty that all the particles of the universe are under his domain and his authority and confess-the stage of constant sacred essence and being the *"Qiyam"* holder of his house of realization, and within the heart, perhaps gradually gets to the point of *"Qiyam"* and the agent oneness, that the learned ones are the secret of which, and comprehend it, then the manifestation stage to the agent manifestation will be revealed to him and the secret of: there is no fatalism and free will, is to be appeared to him then he will become qualified for being present at the presence of God and some of the secrets of the beginning of *takbir* and intonation will

---

[1] *Ilm al-Yaqin*, vol. 2, p. 971.
[2] *Surah Hud*: 112.
[3] *Surah ash-Shawra*: 15.

be revealed to him, hence, after the fixation of this fact in the spiritual's heart, his recitation will be by the tongue of Haqq (Allah), and the praise and the praised will be Allah himself, and some of the secrets of the fate will be exposed to the Gnostic's heart.

and the heart of the Gnostic will receive some of the secrets of the prayer, such as looking at the place of prostration, which is of dust, the principal origin (of man) or subjugating the neck and declining the head, as required, implying humility and destitution of "the possible", and the annihilation under the Might and the Sovereignty of (His) Majesty. "O mankind! It is you who are in need of Allah, and Allah is He who is the Self-Sufficient, the Praised One."[1]

As concerning the wordings of the recitation being a reference to the Unity of Action, we shall explain that in details when we come to comment on the blessed *Surah al-Hamd*, *inshaallah* (Allah willing).

Chapter Three:
[It is on the secrets of intention]

And that is to the common people is to decide to obey: "Who forsake their beds to cry unto their Lord in fear and hope, and spend of that we have bestowed on them."[2]

And to the learned ones it is to decide to obey: "Worship God as if you see him, then if you don't see him, he sees you."[3]

---

[1] *Surah al-Fatir* 35:15.
[2] *Surah as-Sajdah*: 16.
[3] *Bihar al-Anwar*, vol. 74, p. 74.

And to the people of liking and attraction is to decide to obey: Muhammad the prophet said: "The best people are those people who love worshipping."[1]

And he said: "I worship Him because I love Him." And to the holy men is to decide to obey naturally, after the vision of the beloved independently and essentially and annihilated in Lordship essentially and attributably and actually. And due to the utterance of Imam Sadiq: "I worship Allah for His love." Perhaps it is his ordinary stage as our perfect Shaykh used to say: "such worshipping is merely their special ways and is some cases as there some traditions of the messenger (*a*) who said: "I have some special relation that neither angels nor any messenger have had the some or have such capacity."[2]

And there is tradition of Imam Sadiq (*a*): "One day he was performing prayer, he fell and became unconscious, he was asked the reason he replied, I repeated that verse so many times when I heard it myself."[3]

The great Shaykh Shahab ad-Din said: "The tongue of Imam Jafar Sadiq at that time was like the Moses' tree (*a*) that through which God's words was heard." And it seems that the ascension's prayer was so as it is clarified by the tradition.[4]

And it should be known that the intention is the most important cordial duty which is the perfect form of worshipping and it is evaluated according to the deeds, comparing the internal to external, soul to body and the heart to the physical shape. And the most important duty for the whole people is the sincerity hardly any intention can enjoy the real sincerity rather the

---

[1] *Usul al-Kafi*, vol. 3, p. 131.
[2] *Al-Arbain*, p. 177.
[3] *Al-Istilahat*, p. 120.
[4] *Ilal ash-Sharai*, p. 312, ch. 1, tradition 1.

absolute sincerity is the highest point of the holy men—God's good friends—because the sincerity is in fact the purification from the absolute mixing of non-God. And according to the common worship it is the purification of hidden and revealed dualism such as, corruption, hypocrisy, delusion, pride: Surely the pure religion is for Allah only.[1]

And in the purification from the mixing heresy and in the purification of mixing egoism and I-ness which is in the religion of the knowledgeable ones the great dualism and the great heresy: The mother of idols is your desire.[2]

And in related with the God's friends, it is its purification of fermentation vision of obedience and worship, rather vision of the world as Imam Ali (*a*) said: The wise heart is that heart which meets Allah and there in no single spirit is separated from Allah.

Thus, when the spiritual wayfarer stamped out his desires, rather he made himself thoroughly purify, and no sign of anything not seen in his heart and the God's abode were emptied of all idols and released from.[3]

The Satan's plot his religion, his deeds, his inside and outside would be sincere for Allah. And God high and glory, has chosen such religion for himself: Any heart containing doubt and dualism is invalid, and verily chose escapism in this world as their hearts will be released in the hereafter.[4]

---

[1] The troops, 3.
[2] *Mathnawi*, vol. 1, p. 22.
[3] *Usul al-Kafi*, vol. p. 26.
[4] *Usul al-Kafi*, vol. 3, p. 26.

Chapter Four:
[Some discipline and secrets of *takbir*s and the eradication of hands]

Thus, you, the spiritual wayfarer and the fighter on God's way when you decide to stand before the God's presence and the purification of intention and the heart then having entered within the people of faithful ones, prepare yourself for being present at his presence and ask for knocking, leave the nature abode for removing the thick veil through appealing to the divine stage and then throw your hands behind, while calling *takbir* enter the further veil, and pass the third veil in the same way till you get to the favorite destination, stop! And read this supplication Oh God thou art the king of hidden and visible.[1]

Divestment of ownership from but God, and the absolute unlimited possessions, namely another important discipline of the *takbir* is that the *salik* is to strive, and by cordial austerities he is to prepare his heart to be the place for the majesty of Allah, the glorified, and to regard greatness, glory, sovereignty and majesty to be exclusively ascribed to the sacred essence of Allah, the most high, and to exclude the others from majesty. If he feels in his heart even a tiny bit of anyone else's greatness, without taking, it to be the light of that of Allah's his heart is sick and controlled by satan.

And don't consider yourself the exalter of the veil and not to be considered deserve of calling *takbir*: "He is much greater than can be described."[2]

Thus, the *salik*'s attention is first directed to the majesty of the sacred essence according to these general affairs, so at first, he introduces the greatness and majesty to the visible and invisible

---

[1] *Bihar al-Anwar*, p. 206.
[2] *Usul al-Kafi*, vol. 1, p. 159.

powers of his own kingdom. Then, secondly to the angels of Allah in charge of the invisible powers spread in the kingdom of soul. Thirdly, to the begins of the invisible and visible worlds and fairly to the angels of Allah in charge of the kingdom of the heavens and the earths."[1]

Thus the express being weak toward the divinity and ask for being forgiven for the fault and sins you committed. After that unveil the fourth curtain and also the fifth one, repeat *takbir*, open your heart's eyes as to hear "The invitation". And if the sweetness of the presence and the pleasure of entering or the greatness of the presence will be appeared in your heart, you must know that you are allowed to enter, now repeat while being wailing and begging: "My head is at thy command and prosperity is thy and the wickedness has no way toward thee."[2]

And think about the reality of these holy praising in which there are the doors of Gnostics and within there is the discipline of being at the presence after purification and permission of Allah to enter and to be at his presence and the purification of his sacred stage of description, eradicate the sixth veil and call *"takbir"* and if you find yourself qualified for it, eradicate the seventh veil which is the seventh subtlety, otherwise stop, and knock at the God's generosity late and tell sincerely: "Oh the good maker of bad deeds, I have approached Thee." And be aware that you say it truly and be afraid of lying at the presence of God.

And then eradicate the seventh veil by throwing your hands backwards, call *takbir* and separate and deprive yourself from the others as you have been within the limitation of generosity

---

[1] Extracted from *the Discipline of Prayer*, by Imam Khomeini, p. 125-6.
[2] *Bihar al-Anwar*, vol. 81, p. 35.

then say: "They restrained not one another from the wickedness they did. Verily evil was they used to do it."[1]

And be aware that a great risk has been occurred to you that is the disunion at the beginning of the *salat* at the presence of the God. And if, like the writer of these pages being covered of any perfection and knowledge and being connected to the worldly material and being busy in lust and fury you will find yourself deprive from these stages, don't defame yourself at the presence of God and the proximate angels, and confess your faults and defects and be ashamed of your own shortcomings and disobeying and with the broken heart and being regretted enter and say the supplications through the tongue of the holy men because you are not qualified, because unless you disregards the worlds" you won't be believed thereabout, and unless you will be subordinate to Allah you won't be Muslim, and as far as you are selfish, you are within the circle of dualism, and unless you become the absolute annihilated you can not say:

"Say Lo! My worship and my sacrifice and my living and my dying are for Allah, Lord of the worlds."[2]

Thus, if you find yourself unable for such task, never stand in the first row of the people of the knowledgeable and don't make fun of yourself before the nobles.

There is a reference to some of what has been said in a lengthy tradition in *Ilal ash-Sharai*, quoting Imam Jafar (a) describing the ascending. He said: "Allah, the Glorified and Almighty, sent down to the Prophet a carriage of light comprised of forty sorts of light which were around the heaven. The heaven of Allah, Blessed and most high, blurs the eyes of the onlookers. One of them was yellow, and it became the cause of the yellowness of

---

[1] *Surah al-Anam*: 79.
[2] *Surah al-Anam*: 162.

the yellow. Another one was red, and it became the cause of the redness of the red..." Then he added: "... He [the Messenger (*s*)] sat in it and it ascended him to the lower heaven." The angels ran to the outskirts of the heaven, and then they fell in prostration, and said: "All-glorified and All-holy is our Lord, the Lord of the angels and the Spirit. How this light is like the light of our Lord!" Jibrail (Gabriel) said: "God is great!" The angels stopped talking, and the heaven was opened. The angels gathered and came to pay tribute to the Prophet (s) group after group... as the tradition goes.[1]

But about the holy men's prayer—at it was said before—it is the manifestation of reflection, thus when make their own pure heart the scene of the invisible world and their focus their own heart's mirror upon the real sun, for the sake of their heart behalf of the invisible stage an especial manifestation will be occurred to them, and when at first the manifestation is restrictive the call a "*takbir*" then they consider it as the veil's light and divert their heart from it and through their hands show the eradication of the heart's veil. After eradicating the veil another manifestation will occur in their hearts higher than the former one, then they say, and call "*takbir*" and through which eradicate that veil, it goes the same up to the seventh stage-which they eradicate it to reach the ultimate union stage of blessing. And, thus, when the essentials manifestation occurs upon their heart without restrictive and without veil: "Lo, I have turned my face towards Him who created the heavens and the earths as one by nature upright, and I am not of the idolaters"[2] Saying this and enter the prayer and through *takbir* deprive themselves from anything but God and make unlawful anything but God and consider everything the breaker of the prayer and consider them the cutter

---

[1] *Ilal ash-Sharai*, vol. 2, p. 312, sec. on "The Causes of the *wudu*, the *adhan* and the *salat*," *hadith* 1, p. 312.
[2] *Surah al-Anam*: 79.

of the prayer, and when they reach such stage utter: "When we did appoint for…"[1]

And the people of the knowledge say the verse: "When the night grew dark upon him beheld a star which refers to the spiritual journey of Ibrahim and it quality, and to the whatever you have heard: In tradition quoted from Imam Jafar (*a*) who was asked by: Hisham Ibn Hakam: Why at the beginning of the prayer seven *takbir*s have more blessing? He replied: "Oh Hisham, God created seven heavens seven earths, seven veils and when the messenger was ascended and his nearness was as the distance of two heads of a bow, or nearer he took one his veils, the messenger called *takbir* and started calling *takbir* seven times, therefore for the beginning of the prayer seven *takbir*s are called.[2]

From the ascension tradition it will be clarified that for the messenger (*a*) three times the great light have been manifested through the primary *takbir*s, the same case happened for Khalilullah (*a*) then the union achieved and in this tradition also mentions: "Then, when from the primary *takbir* was through God Almighty said: "Now, you have approached me, call my name."[3]

Chapter Five:
[On some of the secrets of recitation]

And for that, like other parts of it, there are some stages and degrees according to the stages of the people of the worship and conduct we recite it briefly:

---

[1] *Surah al-Araf*: 142.
[2] *Ilal ash-Sharai*, p. 332.
[3] *Ilal ash-Sharai*, p. 312.

First; the ordinary recitation that the origin of which is modulation, and the correcting formal form, and its perfection is thinking about the meaning and the conventional conception.

Second, the special recitation, and it is God's reality subtle words within the heart according to the reason's ability or the Gnostic's completion and its completion finds its own expression in some of the secret of the recitation's stages.

Third; the recitation of the knowledgeable ones and it is the translation of their own impression after having realized some of the Quran's reality stages.

Fourth: the recitation of the people of the hearts and it is the translation of the hearts conditions after having realized some of the reality of the Quran's stages.

Fifth: It is the recitation of the holy men and for that there are in brief three stages.

First, the translation's stage of the agent manifestation upon the guardianship, second, the manifestation of the nominal translation, and thirdly the manifestation of the essential translation, and in these three stages the reader praises through the divinity tongue, because the example of supererogatory proximity begins from the agent manifestation stage, thus the wayfarer praises his worship through the tongue of Allah, the servant becomes the God's tongue and God becomes the servant tongue[1] Ali (*a*) said: "Ali is the God's eyes God's hands and tongue."[2]

And for each of these stages there are some degrees too that the description of which is long.

---

[1] *Maani al-Akhbar*, p. 17, tradition 14.
[2] *Maani al-Akhbar*, p. 17, tradition 14.

Connection: When you eradicate the veil and conquer the gates enter the magnanimity and appeal to the sacred great name against Satan, the creator of the perfect man, and call Satan in the true word "Damned devil" and consider it real damned as here it refers to its annihilation. Thus, when you have given up the world and decided to approach, make yourself the addressee of: Now you reach me call me.[1]

Otherwise consider yourself within the soldiers of devil. When you hear the God's order through the insight ears and you are allowed to enter the divinity stage, say *bismillah* and enter.

Chapter Six:
[On the [secret] of *istiadhah*]

And its reality is seeking refuge from Satan and its managements and manifestations to the stage of Allah's Name who is the creator of the perfect man, namely the *salik*'s stage, his real objective is to attain essential perfection and happiness, but there is a Satan with a snare of his snares to prevent him from reaching his objective, the *salik* will have to take refuge in Allah from that Satan and his evils and tricks, thus as long as the *salik* is still within the frame of the soul and the evil of nature the aim of his journey is to attain self perfections and his recitation is through the I-ness and selfish tongue which is the Satan elaborate tongue and whatever the *salik* utters is not the God's name and when *salik* exits out from these branches and finds himself free from such domination and observers the Allah's manifestations within the existing creation, he will achieve the first stage of *istiadhah* of the people of the conducts, and this *istiadhah* is "*qiyam*" and recitation, because both of them are the agent stage of Oneness.

---

[1] *Ilal ash-Sharai*, p. 312.

In other word, to expand this summary as long as man is dwelling in the abode of the self and nature, and has not yet started his spiritual journey and *salik* to Allah, and is still under affairs *istiadhah* and mere utterances of his tongue are useless or rather they fix and strengthen the Satanic authority, unless Allah, the exalted, grants him his favor and recitation. But *qiyam*, as it was foresaid both are the stage of agent *tawhid*. And but recitation after mentioning the guardianship stage and for the people of the guardianship is the realization thereof, and the lowliness to the stage of the will.

But recitation then mentioning the God's name, which is the absolute "Will" and the summary of all praises to God and mentioning the stage of benevolence and mercifulness and the ownership and referring to the *"nabudu"* and *"nastain"* and mentioning the stage of lead to the straight path avoid tendencies to the "extremes" all aspects are to the actions of Oneness as it is clear for the knower.

And when the *salik* exits from the attribute chains and saw the whole names and attributes smash and decreed to annihilate he will be at the stage of *istiadhah* which is the *istiadhah* of prostration and its invocation because prostration and its invocation refers to the stage of oneness of attributes, as we will refer to it, God's will. And when he erases the veil of chains and would abolish the illuminate and dark veil and attained the essentials *"tawhid"* stage and comprehensive annihilation the real *istiadhah* has been achieved, and this *istiadhah* is genuflection and its invocation because at it will be explained it is referred to the stage of essential *"tawhid"*. And it can be referred to the triple stages as it has been narrated by the messenger (*a*) who said while genuflecting:

Be aware that the theologians differ about the relation of *"ba"* in the *"Bismillah"* *ir-rahman ir-rahim*. Each theologian, accordance with his own view, knowledge and Gnosticism has expressed some comment thereabout. For instance the learned theologians connect it to the entry "Beginning" or seeking help. As to some narratives it means: "I seek help" it conforms with the common taste, being so frequent in the traditions and the variety of a lot of traditions is clarified to this attitude and therefore that Imam ar-Rida (*a*) expressed *bismillah* to convey the meaning "I put on myself a "sign" of God's [24] or "Seeking help" conveys too subtle conception to be comprehended by the ordinary people, including the mystery of *tawhid* in a more delicate contact.

Some of the knowledgeable men comment that *bismillah* refers to "appeared" namely: existence appeared by Bismillah.[25] This, conforms with the knowledgeable men of conduct and Gnosticism, uttering that the entire Beings, the particles of existence and the visible and the invisible realm of manifestations of the whole-encompassing Name of God, namely "The supreme Name" of God: The "Greatest Name". Therefore "Name" which means "Sign" and "Mark" or zenith and Altitude is God's effusive and actual manifestation being called "effusive Emanation" and brilliant annexation, for due to this conduct, the entire of house of Realization as from the abstract

From thy punishment I appeal to thy forgiveness and from thy fury to thy satisfaction and from Thee I appeal to Thyself.[1]

And whatever was said in this stage that the *qiyam* and recitation is the agent *tawhid* stage-has no difference with whatever in chapter three, the preface of the secret of prayer-was said that "*iyyaha nabudu*" is the returning of the servant to the Allah toward the absolute annihilation-because for each recitation and prostration and genuflection there is a stage. Thus, *qiyam* to the

---

[1] *Awali al-Laali*, vol. 4, p. 114.

stage of agent *tawhid* has been related, though it possesses the essential *"tawhid"* and the attribute internally. And this the same words as the Gnostic utter about the names, attributes, verbs and essence, though they consider each name as a collective, comprehensive name in which the manifestation of the name is appeared, and the manifestation of the attribute and essential would be therein. And the same in namely attribute and the essential one.

Chapter Seven:
[A glance on the blessed *Surah al-Hamd*]

Abstract intellects down to the lowest degrees of existence are the phenomenalizations of this emanation and the descents of this grace. This conduct is supportable by many noble divine and honorable traditions of the infallible and purified *Ahl al-Bayt* (a), such as the noble tradition in *al-Kafi* which says: "Allah created the will through the will itself, and then He created all the things through will."[1] This honorable tradition is interpreted according to the opinion of each interpreter's creed. The most obvious one is that which is in conformity with the creed saying that "Will" means, here, the Will in action, which is the "Effusive Emanation," and the "thing" is the stages of existence, and which are the phenomena and the descents of this grace. So, the tradition will thus mean that Allah, the Exalted, has created the Will-through the Will itself, without intermediation, and the other creatures of the invisible and visible worlds have been created in the wake of that. Yet, Sayyid Muhaqqiq Damad (may his grave be sanctified), a great scholar and strict researcher as he was, interpreted this noble tradition[2] in a strange way.

---

[1] *Usul al-Kafi*, vol. 1, p. 149, "*Book of at-Tawhid*," ch. on "The will is among the Attributes of Action…," *hadith* 4; *Bihar al-Anwar*, vol. 4, p. 145.

[2] *Mirat al-Uqul*, vol. 2, p. 19; *al-Wafi*, vol. 1, p. 100.

Similarly, the explanation of the late Fayd (may Allah have mercy upon him) is also far from being correct.[1]

However, "Name" is the very manifestation of Act, with which this House of Realization is realized (actualized). The term "Name," referring to real things, is frequently noticed to be used by Allah, His Messenger and the infallible *Ahl al-Bayt*, who said: "We are the Beautiful Names."[2]

In the noble invocations one frequently recites: "By Your Name in which you manifested to so and so.[3]

It is possible that the *bismillah* at the opening of each surah belongs to the same *Surah*. For example, the *bismillah* of the blessed *Surah al-Hamd* belongs to the *Surah* itself. This opinion coincides with the Gnostic taste and the way of the people of knowledge, as it is to say that the praise of the praise and the eulogy of the eulogists point to the self-subsistence of the Name "Allah." Therefore, the *tasmiyah* comes as a preliminary to all words and acts-which is an act of religious supererogation-and it is to remind that whatever word or act done by man is by the self-subsistence of the divine Name, since all the particles of existence are the phenomena of "Allah's Name," and, in a way, they themselves are "Allah's Names". On this basis, the meaning of the *bismillah*, according to the majority, is different in each *Surah*, each word and each act. The jurisprudents say that the *bismillah* must be defined for each *Surah*, that is, if for a *Surah* a *bismillah* was recited, the next *Surah* cannot be commenced with that same *bismillah*. From the juristic point of view, this is not

---

[1] *Al-Wafi*, vol. 1, sec. on "knowing His Attributes and Names, the Glorified," ch. on "The Attributes of the Act," explaining of *hadith* 4, p. 100.

[2] *Usul al-Kafi*, vol. 1, "*Book of at-tawhid*," ch. "Rarities," *hadith* 4, p. 196.

[3] From the noble invocation called *Dua as-Simat*. see *Misbah al-Mutahajjid*, p. 376.

without reason, as, actually, it is reasonable within the scope of this research. But, Allah, all *bismillah*s have a single meaning.

These two opinions are also applied to the stages of existence and the stations of invisibility and visibility. In the view of multiplicity and seeing the phenomena, all the multiplied beings, the stages of existence and the vanishing of multiplicities and the effacement of the lights of existence in the eternal light of the sacred emanation, there is nothing except the sacred emanation and the All-embracing Name of Allah. Both of these two opinions are also present in the divine Names and Attributes. According to the first opinion, the state of Unity is the state of multiple Names and Attributes, as all multiplicities are from Him. According to the second opinion, there is no name and form except the Greatest Name of Allah. These two opinions are wise and thought upon. But if the view became Gnostic through opening the doors of the heart, and through the steps of conduct and cordial austerity, Allah, the Exalted, will appear in the hearts of its possessors through His manifestations in Act, Name and Essence, sometimes in the Attribute of multiplicity and sometimes in the Attribute of Unity. The Glorious Quran refers to these manifestations, both overtly, as in His saying: "And when his Lord manifested (His light) to the mountain, He made it crumble to dust, and Moses fell down senseless,"[1] and covertly, as in the scenes witnessed by Ibrahim (*a*) and the Messenger of Allah (*s*), which are referred to in the *surah*s al-Anam and *an-Najm* as well as in the narratives and the invocations of the infallibles (*a*) which frequently refer to the same topic, especially in the great *dua* [invocation] called "*as-Simat*," whose authenticity and text cannot be denied by the deniers, and it is accepted by both the Sunnis and the Shiahs, and by both Gnostics and common people. In this noble invocation

---

[1] *Surah al-Araf* 7:143.

there are many high meanings and teachings smelling which raptures the Gnostic's heart, and its breeze blows divine breath into the *salik*'s spirit. It says: "By the light of Your Face with which You appeared to the mountain and made it crumble to dust, and Moses fell down senseless; by Your Glory which appeared at the mount of *Tur* of *Sina*, with which You talked to Your rise in *sayr* and Your appearance on the mount Faran..."[1]

In short, the *salik* to Allah has to inform his heart, when reciting the *bismillah*, which all the outward and inward beings and all the visible and invisible worlds, are under the education of the Names of Allah, or rather, they are manifests and stillness, and all the world's are based on the self-existence of the Greatest Name of Allah. So, his praises are for Allah, and his worship, obedience, monotheism, and sincerity are all because of the self-existence of the Name of Allah. It is by intense remembrance, which is the aim of worship, that this state, this divine grace, is established and fixed in his heart, as Allah, the Exalted, in his intimate meeting and sacred assembly, with His interlocutor, said: "Verily I am Allah; there is no god but I; so worship Me and perform the prayer for My remembrance."[2]

The objective of performing the prayer is, He said, to remember Him. After intense remembrance, another way of knowledge will be opened to the heart of the Gnostic and he will be attracted to the world of Unity until the tongue of his heart: "Praise is for Allah by Allah," and "You are as You praised Yourself," and "I take refuge in You from You."

That was a summary of the relation of the "B" in *bismillah*, and some information obtained from it. As to the secrets of the "B", and the dot under the "b" of *bismillah*, which, in its innermost, refers to the *Alawiyan* position of guardianship, and the state of

---

[1] Extracted from the *dua as-Simat, Misbah al-Mutahajjid*, p. 376.
[2] *Surah Ta Ha* 20:40.

the Quranic Collective Union, they need a wider scope to explain.

As regards the truth of the Name, it has an invisible station, an invisible of the invisible, and it has a secret of the secret, a Name is the mark of Allah and is vanished in His Sacred Essence. So, any name which is nearer to the horizon of the Unity, and farther from the world of multiplicity, is more complete in nomination; and the most complete name is that which is innocent from multiplicities, even the multiplicity of knowledge, and that is the invisible manifestation of "*Ahmadiyan* Oneness" in the Essence by the state of the "Holiest Emanation", which may be what was referred to by the noble *ayah*: "...or closer still"[1]. Then there is the manifestation by the greatest Name of Allah in the Unity; then there is the manifestation by the "Holy emanation"; then there are the manifestations by the attributes of multiplicity in the essences, etc. till the last stage of the House of Realization. The writer has already explained this brief in *Misbah al-Hidayah* and in the exegesis of *Dua as-Sahar*.[2]

"Allah" is the state of appearance in the "Holy emanation" if by "Name" the existential individuations are meant, in which are applying "Allah" to it as a union between the manifest and the manifestation, and the vanishing of the Name in the Named, is not objectionable Perhaps, the ayah "Allah is the light of the heavens and the earth,[3] and "And He it is Who in the heaven and in the earth is God,"[4] are a reference to this state, and an

---

[1] "So he was at the measure of two bows or closer still." *Surah an-Najm* 53:9.

[2] The exegesis of *Dua as-Sahar* is of the exudations of the pen of Imam Khomeini (may Allah be pleased with him) in Arabic. The aim of writing it, as the exegete himself says, was to explain some espects of the noble invocation called "*mubahilah*" (The invocation of *Sahar* has been narrated from the pure Imams [a]). The writing of this noble book was completed in 1349, L.H.

[3] *Surah an-Nur* 24:35.

[4] *Surah az-Zukhruf* 43:84.

evidence proving the said application. It is the state of Unity and the Union of the Names. In other words, it is the state of the Greatest Name if by "Name" the state of manifestation by the other possibilities. Or it is the state of the Essence or the state of the "Holiest Emanation" if by "Name" the "Greatest Name" is intended. Consequently, the states of "Beneficent" and "Merciful" are different, according to these possibilities, as is clear.

It is possible that "Beneficent" and "Merciful" are adjectives for "Name" or they may by adjectives for "Allah," but they are more suitable to be adjectives for "Name", because in praising they are adjectives for "Allah," and thus, it will be immune from repetition, although their being adjectives for "Allah" is also justifiable. In repetition there is, however, a point of eloquence. If we take them to be adjectives for "Name" it supports the idea that by "Name" the essential Names are intended, because only the essential Names can bear the adjectives of ?Beneficent" and "Merciful." So, if by "Name" the essential Name and the manifestation in the state of Collectivity are intended, "Beneficent" and "Merciful" will be attributes of the essence, which, in the manifestations by the state of unity, are confirmed for "the Name of Allah," and the mercy of the Beneficent and the Merciful in act is of their demotions and appearances. And if by the "Name" the collective manifestation in act is intended, which is the state of will, the "Beneficence" and "Mercifulness" are attributes of act. So, the mercy of the "Beneficence" is the expanse of the origin of the existence, which is general and for all beings, but it is of the particular attributes of Allah, because in expanding the origin of the existence, Allah, the Exalted, has no partner, and the hands of other beings are short of having the mercy of creating: "There is no effecter in the [world of] existence except Allah, and there is no God in the House of Realization but Allah."

Regarding the mercy of "Mercifulness", of whose exudations is the guidance of the guides on the road, it is especially for the fortunate and the high dispositions, but it is of the general attributes, of which other beings have their share, too, as it has already been explained that the mercy of Mercifulness is of the general mercies, and that the wicked have no share of it because of their own evils, not because of any limitation. Therefore, guidance and invitation are for the entire human family, as is confirmed by the Glorious Quran. However, another opinion says that the mercy of the "Mercifulness" belongs only to Allah, and no one else has any share of it. The noble narratives, taking into consideration the different opinion and estimations also differ in explaining the mercy of Mercifulness. Sometimes it is said: "The Beneficent' is a particular Name for a general Attribute, and the Merciful' is a general Name for a particular Attribute.[1] In another instance it is said: "(He is) Beneficent to all His creatures, and Merciful to the beliefs in particular.[2] It is also said: "O Beneficent of this world and Merciful of the Hereafter",[3] or "O Beneficent and Merciful of this world and the Hereafter."

Chapter Eight:
[Some exegesis of the blessed *Surah at-Tawhid*]

Know that in *bismillah* this verse and its relations, there is the same possibility that there is in the holy verse "*Hamd*" which was mentioned, but in here due to the belonging to the "*qul huwa*" say: "He is Allah, the One."

---

[1] *Majma al-Bayan*, vol. 1, p. 21, quoting Imam Jafar as-Sadiq (*a*), with a slight difference.
[2] *Maani al-Akhbar*, p. 3; *Bihar al-Anwar*, vol. 89, p. 229.
[3] *Usul al-Kafi*, vol. 4, p. 340, "*the Book of the Invocation*," ch. on "Invoking on Calamities," *hadith* 6; *as-Sahifah as-Sajjadiyyah*, Invocation 54.

In the first noble verse of the blessed of *"Hadid"* there are delicate things of *at-tawhid* and great information of the secrets of divinity and abstraction, like of which is unseen in the divine revelations and the book of the people of knowledge and the owners of heart.

Perhaps "He" points to the state of the essence. And, as it is an invisible reference, it is actually a reference to the unknown. "Allah" and *"Ahad"* are references to the state of "Unity" and Oneness.

So, He introduces the essence, and the names of the unitary attributes. In fact, it points to the fact that the essence is invisible and the hands of hopes are short of reaching it, and that spending the life in thinking astray, and that what is known to the people of Allah and to the knowledge of those who know Allah, is related to the states of "Unity" and Oneness, the "Unity" being for the common people of Allah, whereas "Oneness" is for the special people of Allah.

Thus, He refers to the absent stage, as there is in tradition and Allah refers to the Oneness stage which is the supreme name, and from *"Ahad"* till the end of the verse there are the purifications names, thus the holy verse is related to God through all stages, and he can be referred to the essence, the essential names *"wal-ilmu indahu."*

Chapter Nine:
[On some of the secrets of *ruku*]

And that is to the singled out ones that exist from the *qiyam* stage and persisting on servitude and to the knowledgeable people required claiming. And to the liking people is the exit from hypocrisy and criminal stages and entering the stage of supplication, subordination, and abase which is the stage of middle class. [We, in the secret of *salat* hint to these stages in terms of the Gnostic taste, on we explain them in other terms suitable to the common people][1] he hears the praising of God's angels, rather hears all the creatures praising he utters through the God's tongue: "*Samiallah li man hamidah.*"

Then when he stood up and calling "God is great". After prostration he would abolish the multiplicities of names absolutely then become deserve for the proximity stage and intimacy namely the stage's attending.

Chapter Ten:
[Concerning raising the head from the prostration]

Raising the head from the prostration is the return from standing in the multiplicity of names and annihilated in attributes and limiting and stopping in that stages because after the awakening from annihilation in the names the spiritual wayfarer servant witnesses his failure and shortcoming, from the beginning of *ruku*-prostration, he would then stand erect out of this state and with *takbir ruku*, he would remove the multiplicities of names. And when [Thus for being understandable for the common who need to know such discipline precisely preferably we bring the clear and simplified text by Imam Khomeini (*a*) written in the Discipline of the prayer]

Chapter Eleven:
[On secret of genuflection]

And that is to the people of the secret the whole secret of the prayer and the prayer's secret entirely and the last stage of proximity and most ultimate union's point, rather it is not its

---

[1] Imam Khomeini, *the Discipline of Prayer*, p. 350.

follower, is the time when the whole attending toward it, have been cut out and all the tongues are speechless and all speeches are mute from its stage and whoever mentions it is unaware thereabout:

These pretenders searching him are unknowing for those who have known not yet recovered their feelings [Sadi].

And whatever had been said or will be said of the veil's masters, rather it is the means of veil.

The Gnostic researcher, Ansari has said: "But the third stage of oneness is the Oneness which God possesses only and he gained it through his ability and has spread some fraction of it to some of the distinguished singled ones and made them mute and dumb thereabout unable to mention anything entirely. And whatever is being said is only guess. "

Thus, the secret of the position of genuflection is to give up oneself, and the discipline of putting the head on the dust is to debase one's most high position, regarding it to be lower than the dust, should there be in the heart a cause for these claims, in respect of the states of knowledge, hypocrisy. And, as this state is the head on the dust is to debase one's most high position, regarding it to be lower than the dust. Should there be in the heart a cause for these claims, in respect of the states of knowledge, hypocrisy. And as this state is the most dangerous one, the spiritual wayfarer to Allah will have to cling to the skirt of the care of Allah, the most high, by means of his personal disposition and innermost nature, humbly and meekly asking forgiveness for the shortcomings. "But this is a dangerous state that is out of obligations of people like us."[1] And for it, according to the condition of the jurisprudent of Allah there are stages and ranks we will refer to them as follows:

---

[1] *The Discipline of the Prayer*, p. 357 by Imam Khomeini.

One of them is the comprehensive stage which is the stage of jurisprudents and the learned ones through thinking and following the reason and science. And this is the stage of the people of great veil who are the jurisprudents and the knowledgeable ones.

Second, the faith stage and its completion is the trustee and this is the stage of the pious and the faithful ones. Third, the stage of the people of the vision and the people of the heart's who observe the absolute annihilation through the vision light, and the stage of perfect manifest in their hearts.

Fourth, the stage of the people of research and the holy men who achieve the absolute Oneness and the multiplicity and the two bows' length will be removed and through the identity with its all aspects annihilated in formal multiplicity and scattered in formal gathering and vanished within the light and annihilated in divinity and extinct in absent identity. Thus, the self-effacement will be occurred and the perfect unconscious will be achieved and the perfect annihilation will happen and the gloom cover of servitude will be disappeared.

And if the spiritual wayfarer's heart is small and his capacity's stage is short, that it is given due to the manifestation of the sacred emanation he will be remain in the condition of self-effacement and won't return to the sobriety case, perhaps: "My friends are under my domes, no body knows them, (Ibid) is referred to this God's group. But if he possesses a vast heart and deserve becoming the manifestation of sacred emanation in this case the effacement won't remain and from this condition will come into subtle blessing and tranquility and finally into the sobriety, in this stage he will observe God with all aspects of internally and externally and powerfully, and there would be no veil in between. And the spiritual wayfarer if his heart's capacity is small and his rank of ability—due the manifestation of sacred emanation which has been given to him—would be defected, he will remain in the unconscious case and effacement and won't return into the sobriety condition and perhaps: "My holy men are under my domes and nobody knows them but Me,"[1] is referring to these group of God. But if he possesses a vast heart and being attended by the God Almighty's sacred emanation, won't remain in the effacement condition and from this effacement he will return to manifestation of subtle blessing and becomes calm and tranquility and the sobriety after self-effacement will happen to him, and in such situation and stage he will observe Allah will all respects, externally and internally and powerfully, in fact: The genuflection is a swoon and a shock resulting from witnessing the lights of the Greatness of Allah. When the servant feels being ruptured and undergoes a fit of annihilation—effacement—and shock he will be covered by the eternal care and will receive inspiration from the unseen.

And in this stage the wayfarer conduct plays no role at all and the obedience step is cut entirely. therefore the "spiritual Gnostic" refers to these stages and says:

Through worshipping God you may become, but being Moses you will not become. The first part, is referring to the stage of the people of the conducts and the people of union, in which the obedience step plays a role therein, and in the second part it refers to the sobriety condition which is beyond the horizon of obedience entirely, and through the tongue of some the Gnostics is referring to the manifestation of the sacred emanation which says: "All are afraid of the ending I am afraid of the beginning."

And there many traditions about such stage and this is of the great secrets of "fate" about the covering of which the holy men shut their mouths, and are not allowed to talk about it.

---

[1] *Ihya al-Ulum ad-Din*, vol. 4, p. 256.

Shortly effacement has no veil from unseen and vision and their beings are the divinity and they see the world through divinity: "I saw nothing unless".[1]

"Within or with it I saw God."[2] The essentials manifestation, nominal manifestation and the agent manifestation, none of them, won't cover each other, rather in essential manifestation. The agent and the attribute manifestation are seen too; similarly in essential manifestation the manifestation of an agent and attribute ones are seen. And referring to whatever we have said: in tradition "the prayer of ascension" says." Then said: "Raise your head", I raised my head, I saw something that due to which I went mad, I lay on the soil through my hands and my face, then I was inspired through the exaltation whatever I saw, I said: *Subhana rabbi*—pure is the God praising deserves Thee.

I repeat seven times, I came over but each time I uttered I fainted, then I sat down, therefore the invocation: Pure is God... occurred in genuflection.

Oh God, what secret there is unable to write about it and the tongue cannot express anything thereabout. This great light that he observed while prostrating and fainted, whatever he saw after prostration, that even did not compare and mention it as greatness, whether it was of the essential names or the manifestation of unveiled names? Whether the repetition of the exaltation had any aim of submission or any other secrets. And whether the God's inspiration while the (wayfarer) was unconscious what sort of name it enjoyed that result of which admitting and describing to the exaltation which is the first essential names that Allah chose it for himself and the praising which is the means of manifestation to the multiplicity, God knows!

---

[1] It meant Khwajah Abdullah Ansari.
[2] *Ilm al-Yaqin*, vol. 1, p. 54.

It is stated in *Misbah ash-Shariah* that Imam as-Sadiq (*a*) said: "By Allah he will not be a loser, the one who performs the *sujud* as it really should be, even if for a single time in his life. No one will be successful if he takes to privacy with his Lord, in a similar position resembling the deceiver of him, unaware of, and neglecting, what Allah has arranged for the *sajjidin* (the prostrate worshippers) of immediate intimacy and adjourned comfort. The one, who is good at the one who observes not the discipline of, and loses the respect for, the *sujud*, can never be near Him by longing for other than Him in his *sujud*. So, let yours be the *sujud* of a submissive and humble to Allah, The Exalted, knowing that you have been created from the dust which is trodden upon by the creatures, and that He has made you of a *nutfah* (semen) which is regarded filthy by everybody, and was brought into existence though not existed before. The concept of the *sujud* has been made by Allah, the Exalted, a cause for getting near Him with the heart, the inside and the spirit. So, whoever nears Him turns away from other than Him. Do you not realize that in the external form the position of the *sujud* is not complete except by hiding oneself from everything, and turning away from all things visible to the eyes? Similar is the question of the internal position. Whoever his heart is attracted, during the *salat*, to other than Allah, the Exalted, he will be near to that which attracted him, and far from the reality of that which Allah wanted him to be in his *salat*. Allah, the Exalted says: "Allah has not made for any man two hearts within him,"[1]

Think of this holy tradition, and don't like the prayers of the God's people to our prayers. The reality of being absolutely with God finds it expression in being absolutely separated with otherness, even desire which is the greatest aliens and the thickest veil. And as long as the man is busy with himself

---

[1] *Surah al-Ahzab* 33:4.

neglects Allah, leave out about being in private state with God! And if in on genuflection in the man's entire life, enjoys a private state with Allah in a real form it makes up all the shortcomings which have been neglected in so many years, the God's grace will help him and he will get rid of the circle of Satan. And while genuflecting which is the stage for eradication I-ness and egoism, the heart would think of something but God, he will become one of the disobey elite.

We seek refuge to God Almighty against the plots of Satan and for the shortcomings and defames and defects to the Lordships' stage. And whatever for the prostration has become blessing is the pleasure of intimacy with the beloved in this world, that for the pious is the best, and in the hereafter it is the revealing the covers and veils and gaining the special blessings which is the main point of the holy men.

Now, we the miserable ones and the wonderer of the wretched abode and intoxicated from the cup of negligence and selfishness have been deprived from the prayers of the people of genuflection and the learned and the people of the hearts. We had better remember our fault, our sins, our shortcomings our indigence our weakness and for our negligence feel sorry and for our covering feel flaming and for such shortcomings and defect and being dominated by Satan would seek refuge to God Almighty perhaps some urgent state would be happened and that sacred essence rescued these miserable wretched ones and fulfills their supplications:

"Is not he (best) who answereth the wronged one he crieth unto Him and removeth the evil?"[1] Thus with the sorrowful and regretted heart let's put our head upon the abased soil which is our origin creature and recall and remember our miserable

---

[1] *Surah an-Naml*: 62.

conditions and through the heart's tongue ask for compensation of our defects and shortcomings from the God Almighty who is our Lord and remember our miserable conditions and through the heart's tongue ask for compensation of our defects and shortcomings from the God Almighty who is our Lord and say to Him, "Oh great God! We have covered within the dark veils of the nature world and big dualism whimsical desires and selfishness and there is Satan within the corner of our bodies, in our blood and veins, and all our limbs are under Satan's control, and against such powerful enemy we appeal to thee only to thy sacred essence, we have no other remedy but you. Thou help us and make our hearts attend toward thyself. Oh God, our attending toward the otherness is not due to the sarcasm, but it is shortcomings, defect of our hearts, our covered hearts made us away from you, and it were not your chastity and refuge we would remain in our cruelty for ever without having any remedy. "O' God! What are we?" David the messenger said: "If there would not be thy chastity I will disobey thee."

There is in tradition that: "When the divine word *Sabaha Rabika ala* was sent the messenger (*a*) said: "Put it in your genuflection." And in *Kafi* tradition it has been mentioned: The first name which God chose for Himself was *"al-ala" al-azim."* And perhaps this nature exaltation which is in the stage of the essential names in the stage of *"ahadiyyat"* is the pure to the people of knowledge, and praising in this stage is the divinity purification of the nominal multiplicities. And the Lordship stage is the divinity to the sacred emanation to which the great Shaykh has referred when he says: *"wal-qabilu min faydihi al-aqdas."*[1]

Thus, the outcome of genuflection is invocation of genuflection to the holy men praising from multiplicities to oneness and attention to essential Lordship which is the result of

---

[1] Muhy ad-Din Arabi.

manifestation to the sacred emanation and seek refuge to the "*al-awal al-aliyy al-ala*" and praising and description entirely through the essential tongue in the *ahadiyyat* stage reflecting upon the mirror. And tranquility in this stage is the submission of this stage, as the eradication head is also submission and the intimacy of another manifestations. And the tranquility of this stage is the man's perfect completion:

"Lo: I have put my trust in Allah, my Lord and your Lord. Not at animal but He doth grasp it by the forelock! Lo, my Lord is on a straight path."

Chapter Twelve:
[On the discipline of the *tashahhud* and *salam*]

Know that as the genuflection on soul is returning to multiplicities without veil practically, *tashahhud* and *salam* is returning to verbally and mention. Therefore in *tashahhud*, first of all testifying is to divinity and oneness and negating the partner for which, pointing all praising to God Almighty merely.

When the *salik* comes out of the state of genuflection—whose secret is annihilation and comes to himself and to a state of wakefulness and attentiveness returning from the state of being absent from the world to the state of being present, and the returning of the praiser entirely to the sacred essence "God's great name". So as he returns he sends peace upon the noble prophet because after returning from unity to multiplicity the first manifestation will be that of the truth of guardianship. Thus, it is the returning of the spiritual wayfarer to himself and asking for health for himself and the devotee servants from returning of this hazardous journey: "Peace on me the day I was born, and the day I die, and the day I shall be raised alive" [1] and this "*salam*" is

---

[1] *Surah Maryam*: 33.

returning from the real death, then is focused upon the God's angels and the messengers and the heaven's soldiers who accompanied him while ascending and asking God for their health, the returning from this spiritual journey as there is in tradition prayer of ascension:

"Suddenly I turned my face I saw so many rows of angels, messengers, the I was told: "Oh Muhammad send regard, I said: *As-salamu alaykum wa rahmatullahi wa barakatuh*". Then, he said: Oh Muhammad verily I am peace and regard you are grace and blessing and you offspring's too.[1]

Perhaps the God's hint is referring to this verse:

"And the earth shineth with the light of her Lord and the book is set up, and prophets the witnesses are brought, and it is judged between them with truth, and they are not wronged."[2]

And the reality of save in this spiritual journey is that the spiritual wayfarer would be away from the desire and I-ness, and if he is saved in this stage, in the second stage in which the divinity blessing would be allotted him, he enjoys a safety state and that safety is attending to the right and avoid attending to the left which is the origin of veils and crookedness.

It is stated in *Misbah ash-Shariah* that Imam as-Sadiq (*a*) said: "The *tashahhud* is extolment of Allah, the most high. So, be his servant in your inside and submit to him in your act, as you are his servant in (your) saying and claim. Join the truthfulness of your tongue to the purity of the truthfulness of your inside, as he has created you a servant and ordered you to worship him with your heart, tongue and organs, and to carry out your servitude by his being your Lord, believing that he has in his grip all the creatures so, they take no breath nor a glance except by his

---

[1] *Ilal ash-Sharai*, p. 312.
[2] *Surah az-Zumar*: 69.

power and will, and they are incapable of performing the least act in his domain except by his permission and will. Allah, almighty and glorious, says: "And your Lord creates what he wills and chooses. They have not the choice Glorified is Allah and Exalted above all that they associate (with Him)."[1] So, be a thankful servant by act, as you are a remembering servant by word and claim. Join the truthfulness of your tongue to the purity of the truthfulness of your inside, for he has created you. He is high above being volition and will to anybody except with his judgment, and uses worship to perform his commands. He has ordered you to send blessing upon his prophet (s). So, join blessing him to blessing him, and obeying him to obeying him and testifying him to testifying him. Take care not to miss the blessings of admitting his sanctity, in which care you will be deprived of the benefit of his blessings, as he ordered him to ask forgiveness for you and intercede for you, if you performed your concerning the obligatory and the forbidden acts, the laws and good manners, knowing his great position with Allah, almighty, most high."[2]

If he stands to servitude all the factors with him will stand. Then, first of all heart should be mentioned by the tongue and finally tongue and any other limbs play the interpreter role of the heart. After that, following the tradition the order for thanking is being issued, and afterwards the stage of satisfaction is dictated that each one has a long debate out of the scope of these pages. And about the important factor of the prayer the knowledge and sending peace to messenger (a) that the spiritual wayfarer should make his heart understand if the entire discovery of that highly stage had not been, no body would have acquainted with the ascension and the union to the proximity stage and as the

---

[1] *Surah al-Qasas* 28:68.
[2] *Misbah ash-Shariah*, ch. 17, on "*The tashahhud.*"

infallible were companions from the beginning of the prayer they should be recalled at the end of the prayer and it should be said that they were the holy men who prepared the means for union to the God's sacred stage: "If they had not existed, the God Almighty would not have been known."

Anyone knows some parts of the reality of guardianship and prophethood he will know how is the relations of the infallible to the people and we thank God in *Misbah al-Huda* have explained about it.

But referring to the secret of *tashahhud* as we mentioned he said: *Tashahhud* is the God's praising" and such subtle point is referred to the realization stage to the sobriety after effacement which the multiplicity of veil—the beloved veil—would not exist and his authority and his will, would infiltrated to all aspects of creation affairs. And this allowance which has been mentioned in the holy tradition is infiltrating from inter to external part. And in this stage the secret of "fate" and the reality of "*amr bayn amrayn*" in the whole course essential, attributable and the agent trends has been visible upon the wayfarer's heart, that the scope of these pages has no room therefore.

It is stated in *Misbah ash-Shariah* that Imam as-Sadiq (*a*) said: "The meaning of the *salam* at the end of each *salat* is "security" that is, whoever obeys the command of Allah and the tradition of His Prophet (*s*), with a submissive heart, will be secured from the trails of this world and exempted from the tortures of the Hereafter. "*Salam*" is one of the names of Allah, the Exalted. He trusted it to His creatures so annexations, exemplifying reciprocal companionship among themselves and the correctness of their association. If you wish to use the *salam* in its proper place and according to its meaning, you must fear Allah, and your religion, heart and mind should be secured on your part. So, do not make them filthy by the darkness of sinning, and do not cause your protectors (angels) to be vexed, tired and disgusted with your maltreating them. Both your friend and, your enemy should be secured from you, as the one whose close friends are not secured from him, the strangers are certainly more expected not to be so. And whoever does not put the *salam* in those proper places, his will be no *salam* and no *taslim*, and his *salam* will be a false one, even if he shows it off before the people.[1]

And in this holy tradition it is referring slightly to the secret of *salam*, and its discipline and the realization of which as follows: But its secret—as it was mentioned—is asking for safety and secured in returning from the journey, that the secured is within the holy men means lack of veil to the beloved through the multiplicity veil which is the utmost degree of the friends' torture, as the Sayyid of the holy men says: "Oh God, supposing I can stand thy torture, how can I stand thy separation?"[2] And for the God's lover no torture is like the pain of separation. Then, the holy men's peace is the secured against the dark veil of the world and the hereafter's veil that each of them is like hard torture.

But about the realization of reality is that point which says, "*Salam* is one the names of Allah. He trusted to it to his creatures. The *salik* servant should declare this dealings, association, trust, and relationships and spread it throughout inside and outside domains.

As far as the man is within the Satan multiplicity veil and his heart is under the enemy's control can not observe the nominal stage and the Lordship's pleasure within himself would talk and observes the world, the world of peace and the manifestation of peace and sees the hands of the traitors short from hypocrisy then he sees the entire being and the world drawn within the

---

[1] *Misbah ash-Shariah*, ch. 18, "On *salam*": *Bihar al-Anwar*, vol. 82, p. 307.
[2] *Kumayl* supplication.

name of "*as-salam*", and in this stage he will find out the perfect secret of the fate secrets. And if through the scientific and theoretical step reveals the secret utterance of the jurisprudents: "*al-wujudu khayrun mahd*" and if he is of the people of Gnostic and discovers, he gains in his heart secured and blessings according to his heart's capacity, God knows. But its disciplines need no description.

The Last Connection:
[On the secrets of prayer]

From whatever has been said—about the secret of the prayer—the reality of which is spiritual wayfaring to and from God—in secret of prayer the other matter will be clarified. And that is when the spiritual wayfarer while genuflecting, the absolute absent from all the creatures will happen to him and will be absent from all the creatures and at the end of genuflection he becomes sober and in *tashahhud* this condition increases, suddenly from being absent of the people the case of being at the presence occurs to him and at the end of the *tashahhud* he pays attention to the prophet hood stage and at his presence performs the needed discipline namely the oral peace. And then through the determination of the guardianship's light which is the internal and external powers of him and the other devotees he will perform the attendant discipline. And then pays attention to the absolute multiplicity absent and testimony and performs the discipline orally and the "*rabi*" journey "*min al-khalq ilal-khalq.*" And this summary needs more explanation that I am unable to say and the people to hear. I am dumb, the world deaf, I saw a DREAM,
I am unable to describe it to the deaf people of the REALM.